Such Respectful Wordful Offerings

Selected Essays Of David Myatt

Edited by Rachael Stirling

Volume One

Contents

- Editorial Preface
- Bright Berries, One Winter
- The Leaves Are Showering Down
- Perhaps Words Are The Problem
- A Non-Terrestrial View
- Musings On Suffering, Human Nature, And The Culture of Pathei-Mathos
- Blue Reflected Starlight
- A Slowful Learning, Perhaps
- Toward Humility – A Brief Personal View
- A Catholic Still, In Spirit?
- Some Personal Perceiverations
- Twenty Years Ago, Today
- Some Questions For DWM, 2017
- Cantio Arcana

Appendix I - A Note On Greek Terms In The Philosophy Of Pathei-Mathos
Appendix II - On Translating Ancient Greek
Appendix III - Concerning ἀγαθός and νοῦς in the Corpus Hermeticum
Appendix IV - Cicero On Summum Bonum
Appendix V - Swan Song Of A Mystic
Appendix VI - Self-Dramatization, Sentimentalist, Or Chronicler Of Pathei Mathos?

"I am still learning, and still striving - and so often failing - each day to live as I feel I should, as an honourable, compassionate, tolerant, person wordlessly aware of and appreciative of the numinous."
David Myatt, 2017

Editorial Preface

This compilation of essays arose out of some enquiries sent or forwarded to us following our re-publication of *Some Questions For DWM, 2017* and of Ms Stirling's article - titled *Swan Song Of A Mystic* - commenting on those questions and answers. Included here are all of the Myatt texts enquired about, plus a few others for context including those 2017 'questions and answers' and *Swan Song Of A Mystic*. We also include an essay - *Self Dramatization, Sentimentalist, Or Chronicler Of Pathei Mathos?* - which takes a critical look at Myatt's post-2010 writings.

Most of the Myatt texts are extracts from David Myatt's correspondence with friends or academics or enquirers, often in response to particular questions asked. All the items included here were published by him under the liberal Creative Commons Attribution-NoDerivatives License which allows for copying and re-publication. All of the translations, quotations, and footnotes are by Myatt.

The texts date from between 2010 and 2017 and are not in any particular order, chronological, by subject, or otherwise. Given the date range there is inevitably some overlap of content and/or of quotations. Considering the development of his weltanschauung between the aforementioned dates, readers may notice how some of his views have evolved; and why - as he noted in one of the more recent texts here - there will be no more personal writings from him

> "because I have become ever more aware of the consequences of words, of my own fallibility; of the depth of my uncertitude of knowing; of how words - including mine - can and often do obscure the wordless empathic essence; and especially aware of how such essays can be, and in my case seem to have been, manifestations of vanity and occasionally of hubris, [with their being] a renewed acceptance of such greater solitude as will hopefully prevent me from any further pontifications public and private, with my translations, slowly proceeding as they are, becoming my only occasional vainful presence in the outer world, for such translations are somewhat other-worldly, and neutral at least in respect of opinions about matters which I now accept are beyond my purview, with my much self-vaunted 'diverse experience over decades' no longer seeming to me to be a viable excuse for inflicting my presumptions and intimations on others."

The title of the compilation is taken from Myatt's translation of the Cantio Arcana of tractate XIII of the Corpus Hermeticum and which 'Esoteric Song' we include here.

Three Wyrd Sisters
2017 ev

Bright Berries, One Winter

Winter, three days before that celebration that marks a certain birth.

Et hoc vobis signum: Inveniétis infántem pannis involútum, et pósitum in præsépio. Et súbito facta est cum Angelo multitúdo milítiæ cæléstis, laudántium Deum, et dicéntium: Glória in altíssimis Deo, et in terra pax homíinibus bonæ voluntátis.

Outside, snow, and a cold wind below a clouded sky - and, there, that partly snow-covered bush of bright berries which hungry Thrushes eat to perhaps keep themselves alive. So many Thrushes, in one place: nine, eleven, gathering on the bare if snowy branches of a nearby taller tree, to descend down to feed, three, five, four, at a time.

Inside, musick - reproduced by some modern means. Musick over five centuries old, bringing such a strange melding of feeling, dreams, memory, and thought. Musick, by Dunstable - *Preco preheminencie*, perhaps one of the most beautiful pieces ever written, bringing thus deep personal feelings.

Now, I cannot seem to help the tears that seep slowly forth (again) from closing eyes, as - far beyond such bounds as causal Time keeps us moving - I am replete, overflowed by memories from such lifeful strange lives as have lived me, here:

> ... there, as she my Sue lay so softly breathing in her bed, my hand to her hand, to watch her sleep to seep hour-long-slowly there past the ending of her life...

> There, as another love from another life that lived me ran, freshly seeping forth from train, along that crowded platform to leap to welcoming arms while people stared, some smiling, and the warmth of bodies touching announced the ending of our exile, of that month of her travelling...

> There, one monk - with such profusion of faith as so infused me then - who knelt, kneels, after Compline in that lovely Chapel before carved centuries-old statue of the Blessed Virgin Mary, feeling such peace as led me back in such respectful reposeful silence to that my cell to sleep dreamless, content...

> Before other lives came to so sadly betake that boyish man away, back to his addiction to such suffering-causing abstractions as would, decades, later, almost break him as she - my Frances of eighteen months together - so then suffused with such tragic fullsome sadness-regret-despair that her slim delicate fingers, no longer to tenderly warmly touch her lover's face, became transformed: a means to betake her, alone lonely, past the ending of her life after I had so selfishly left her that one MayMorn...

So many tears, each some memory seeping sadly joyfully poignantly forth even as so many wait, waiting, ready to heave forth; dormant, seeds needing to bring hence new life as each new Spring becomes some youthful ageing deedful wordful presencing of this one life which is my life until such Time as this emanation also passes beyond that fated Ending who lies in wait to take us all.

Thus am I humbled, once more, by such knowing feeling of the burden made from my so heavy past; so many errors, mistakes. So many to humble me here, now, by such profusion as becomes prehension of centuries past and passing, bringing as such a passing does such gifts of they now long beyond life's ending who crafted from faith, feeling, experience, living, love, those so rich presents replete with meaning; presenting thus to us if only for a moment - fleeting as Thrush there feeding - that knowing of ourselves as beings who by empathy, life, gifts, and love, can cease to be some cause of suffering.

For no longer is there such a need - never was there such a need - to cause such suffering as we, especially I, have caused. For are not we thinking thoughtful beings - possessed of the numinous will to love?

But my words, my words - so unlike such musick - fail: such finite insubstantial things; such a weak conduit for that flowing of wordless feeling that, as such musick, betakes us far out beyond our causal selves to where we are, can be, should be, must be, the non-interfering beauty of a moment; a sublime life seeking only to so gently express that so gentle love that so much faith has sometimes so vainly so tried to capture, express, and manifest; as when that boyish man as monk past Compline knelt in gentleness to feel to become such peace, such a human happiness, as so many others have felt centuries past and present, one moment flowing so numinously to another.

No need, no Time - before this one weakful emanation ends, in ending - to berate, condemn, such love, need and faith as may betake so many in just three days to celebrate such birth as touched, touches, them, and others still. So much good, gentleness, there, and from; and so much suffering, caused, while the centuries past, leeching, meshed one suffering to another.

Does the numinous, presencing, there, now outweigh such suffering, caused - as I, my past, might must outweigh what wordful presents Fate begifts me, now?

I do not know: only see the emanations, nexing, melding: a bush of berries to keep life alive through Winter. Our choice, our need - here, now; as the Thrushes there have no choice, now, as mid-Winter came to bleaken with snowy cold that world that is their world.

For it is for us, surely, to treasure such gifts, given - to feel then be the gift, given.

David Myatt
22 December 2010

The Leaves Are Showering Down

The leaves, having lost most of their green, are showering down in the breeze that, Autumnal-cold, sways the tops of the trees here where the well-trodden almost straight path leads up from the small sea-cliffs, across a narrow local road, and toward an ancient settlement abandoned so very long ago that only a few undulations and mounds remain on the summit of this hill.

Sufficient daylight now to sit on what remains of a fallen tree and type, on a wondrous modern device, such words as this, recalling as I do that

> If you came this way,
> Taking any route, starting from anywhere,
> At any time or at any season,
> It would always be the same: you would have to put off
> Sense and notion. You are not here to verify,
> Instruct yourself, or inform curiosity
> Or carry report. You are here to kneel
> Where prayer has been valid. [1]

For there is certainly a reverence here, within me, as the trees - many far older than I - prepare for their Winter sleep and where a sense of aeonic continuity is felt then known: how many humans would have gathered three millennia ago on such a hill as this to mark - perhaps with bonfire, offerings to their gods, a wordless prayer - the ending of one earthly-season and the beginning of another?

Such continuity, such passing ages; such a knowing of how this hill, that sea, this land - how even many of the trees - will outlive me; combining to bring that perspective which, or so it seems to me, is the root of human humility, burgeoning forth as such humility has (at least according to my fallible understanding) in so many religions and spiritual ways millennia following millennia.

Prayer was - is - valid here. Whatever the gods, the goddesses, the god; however the numen was sensed to be so presenced:

> ἐν τῷ κόσμῳ ἦν καὶ ὁ κόσμος δι' αὐτοῦ ἐγένετο καὶ ὁ κόσμος αὐτὸν οὐκ ἔγνω [2]

So I send this, these words: for there is life within me yet, despite various rumours to the contrary; a solitary life, as is my wish, devoted as it is now and will be, for however long it is gifted to remain, with a gentle desire to complete my translation of the Gospel of John: a meagre offering [3], an expiatory prayer born of an oath I bound myself with on learning of Francine's untimely death ten years ago last May.

As for such rumours, whatever their source, whatever their intent, I am rather reminded of what Sophocles wrote more than two thousand years ago now:

τὸν ἐναγῆ φίλον μήποτ᾽ ἐν αἰτίᾳ σὺν ἀφανεῖ λόγῳ σ᾽ ἄτιμον βαλεῖν [4]

But, as the Sun begins to shed its light within the trees, cold hands and feet remind me to betake myself away to where books await such reading as marks another translating day.

David Myatt
November 5th, 2016

∘∘∘

[1] TS Eliot, Little Gidding

[2] Κατά Ἰωάννην, 1:10. "He who was of the world with the world presenced in him but whose own did not recognize him."

[3] http://www.davidmyatt.info/gospel-john.html [accessed August 2017]

[4] Oedipus Tyrannus, vv.655-6. "When a comrade is under oath, you should never accuse him because of unproved rumours and brand him as being without honour."

Perhaps Words Are The Problem

Of the many metaphysical things I have pondered upon in the last five or so years, one is the enigma of words. More specifically, of how nomen - a name, a term, a designation - can not only apparently bring-into-being abstractions (and their categories) but also prescribe both our thinking and our actions, with such abstractions and such prescription so often being used by us, we mortals, to persuade, to entreat, to manipulate, to control, not only ourselves but through us others of our human kind. Whence how denotatum can and so often does distance, distract, us from the essence - the physis - that empathy and its wordless (acausal) knowing can reveal and has for a certain mortals so often in past millennia revealed.

For we seem somehow addicted to talk, to chatter - spoken and written - just as we assume, we believe, so often on the basis of nomina that we expand our pretension of knowing beyond the local horizon of a very personal wordless empathy breeding thus, encouraging thus, such hubris as has so marked our species for perhaps five thousand years. With such hubris - such certitude of knowing - being the genesis of such suffering as we have so often inflicted on others and, sometimes, even upon ourselves.

Would that we could, as a sentient species, dispense with nomen, nomina, and thus communicate with others - and with ourselves - empathically and thus acquire the habit of acausal wordless knowing. There would then be no need for the politics of propaganda and the rhetoric of persuasion; no need - no ability - to lie or pretend to others. For we would be known - wordlessly revealed - for who and what we really are. And what a different world that would be where no lie, no deception, would work and where guilt could never be concealed.

For some, a few mortals, such a wordless knowing is already, and has been for centuries, the numinous reality, born as such a personal reality is either via their pathei-mathos or via their innate physis. Which is perhaps why such others often secrete, or desire to secrete, themselves away: an isolated or secluded family - rural, or island - living, perhaps, and perhaps why Cistercians, some mystics, some artists, and others of a similar numinous kind, have saught to dwell, to live, in reclusive or communal silence.

There is - or so there seems to me to be according to my admittedly, fallible, uncertitude of knowing - a presencing of the essence of almost all religions here in such a knowing of the value, the mysterium, of silence. Of that which we so often in our hubris forget, have forgotten, or never known: that wordless, that empathic, that so very personal acausal knowing, that personal grief and personal suffering - that the personal awareness of the numinous - so often engenders, so often breeds, as has been so recounted for millennia in our human culture of pathei-mathos.

Given this culture - so accessible now through institutions of learning, through printed books, through art, memoirs, and music, and via this medium of this our digital age - shall we, can we, learn and apply the learning of that culture to significantly change our lives, thus somehow avoiding that periodicity of suffering which for millennia our hubris, our certainty of knowing born of nomen and nomina and the resultant abstractions, has inflicted and continues to inflict upon us?

I do so wish I had an answer. But for now, all I can do is dwell in hope of us en masse so evolving that such empathy, such wordless knowing, has become the norm.

David Myatt
2016

A Non-Terrestrial View

Several times, in the last decade or so, I have - when considering certain current events, and social change, and the activities, policies, and speeches, of certain politicians - often asked myself a particular question: What impression or what conclusions would a non-terran (a hypothetical visiting alien from another star-system) have of or draw from those events, such social change, and those politicians? And what, therefore, would be the conclusions that such a non-terran would make regarding our nature, our human character, as a species?

Which answers seemed to me to depend on what criteria - ethical, experiential, ontological, and otherwise - such a non-terran might employ. Would, for instance, the home-world of such a non-terran be a place of relative peace and prosperity which, having endured millennia of conflict and war, had evolved beyond conflict and war and had also ended poverty? Would, for instance, such a non-terran view matters dispassionately, having evolved such that they are always able to control - or have developed beyond - such strong personal emotions as now, as for all of our human history, so often still seem to overwhelm we humans leading us and having led us to be selfish, to lie, to cheat, to manipulate, to use violence - and sometimes kill - in order to fulfil a personal desire?

The criteria I now (post-2011) apply to this hypothetical scenario are those derived from my own experience, and from reflecting over several years upon that experience, which criteria are of course subjective, personal, and it is thus no coincidence that they now are reflected in my philosophy of pathei-mathos. Thus the ethics I assume such an interstellar space-faring sentient non-terran might adhere to are based on honour and the apprehension of suffering and hubris that empathy provides; just as the ontology derives from a numinous awareness of how causal and fallible and transient every sentient life is in respect of the vastness of the cosmos (spatially and in terms of aeons of causal time), with such ethics and ontology a natural consequence of such a culture whose genesis is that pathei-mathos - ancestral, individual, societal - that derives from millennia of suffering, conflict, war, poverty, and oppression.

Furthermore, my reflexion on the past fifty years of human space exploration leads me to further conclude that we as a species - and perhaps every sentient species - can only venture forth, en masse, to explore and colonize new worlds when certain social and political conditions exist: when we, when perhaps every sentient species, have matured sufficiently to be able to, as individuals, control ourselves (without any internal or external coercion deriving from laws or from some belief be such belief ideological, political, or religious) and thus when we use reason and empathy as our raison d'etre and not our emotions, our desires, our egoism or some -ism or some -ology or some faith that we accept or believe in or need. For despite the technology making such space exploration and colonization now feasible for us (if only currently within our solar system) we lack the political will, the social desire, the trans-national cooperation, the vision, to realize it even given that our own habitable planet is slowly undergoing a transformation for the worse wrought by ourselves. All we have - decades after the landings on the Moon - are a few individuals inhabiting and only for a while just one Earth-orbiting space station and a few small-scale, theorized, human landings on Mars a decade or more in the future. For instead of such a vision of a new frontier which frontier a multitude of families can settle and which can be the genesis of new cultures and new human societies, all we have had in the past fifty years is more of the same: regional wars and armed conflicts; invasions, violent coups and revolutions; violent protests, the killing and imprisonment and torture of protestors and dissenters; political propaganda for this political cause or that; exploitation of resources and of other humans; terrorism, murder, rape, theft, and greed.

How then would my hypothetical space-faring alien judge us as a species, and how would such a non-terran view such squabbles - political, social, ideological, religious, and be they violent or non-violent - and such poverty, inequality, corruption, and oppression, as still seem to so bedevil almost all societies currently existing on planet Earth?

In addition, how would we as individuals - and how would our governments - interact with, and treat, such an alien were such an alien, visiting Earth incognito, to be discovered? Would we treat such an alien with respect, with honour: as a non-threatening ambassador from another world? Would any current government on Earth willingly and openly and world-wide acknowledge the existence of such extra-terrestrial life and allow Earth ambassadors from any country, and scientists, and the media, full and open access to such an alien sentient being? I have my own personal intuition regarding answers to such questions.

But, remaining undiscovered, what would our visiting alien observer report regarding Earth and ourselves on their return to their own planet? Again, I have my own personal intuition regarding answers to such questions. Which answers could well be that we are an aggressive, still rather primitive and very violent, species best avoided until such time as we might outwardly demonstrate - through perhaps having numerous peaceful, cooperating, colonies on other worlds - that we have culturally and personally, in moral terms, advanced.

Which rather - to me at least - places certain current events, social change by -isms, by -ologies through disruption and violence and via revolution, and the activities, policies, and speeches, of certain politicians, and armed conflicts, into what I intuit is a necessary cosmic, non-terran, perspective. Which perspective is of us as a species still evolving; as having the potential and now the means to further and to consciously, and as individuals, to so evolve.

Will we do this? And how? Again, my answer - fallible as it is, repeated by me as it hereby is, and born as it is from my own pathei-mathos - is that it could well begin with us as individuals consciously deciding to change through cultivating empathy and viewing ourselves and our world in the perspective of the cosmos. Which perspective is of our smallness, our fallibility, our mortality, and of our appreciation of the numinous and thus of the need to avoid the error of hubris; an error which we mortals, millennia following millennia, have always made and which even now - even with our ancestral world-wide culture of pathei-mathos - we still commit day after day, year after year, and century after century, enshrined as such hubris seems to be in so many politicians; in -isms and -ologies; in disruptive and violent social change and revolutions; in armed conflicts, and in our very physis as human individuals: an apparently unchanged physis which so motivates so many of us to still be egoistic, to lie, to cheat, to steal, to murder, to manipulate, to be violent, and to often be motived by avarice, pride, jealousy, and a selfish sexual desire.

As someone, over one and half-thousand years ago, wrote regarding human beings:

> τοῖς δὲ ἀνοήτοις καὶ κακοῖς καὶ πονηροῖς καὶ φθονεροῖς καὶ πλεονέκταις καὶ φονεῦσι καὶ ἀσεβέσι πόρρωθέν εἰμι, τῷ τιμωρῷ ἐκχωρήσας δαίμονι, ὅστις τὴν ὀξύτητα τοῦ πυρὸς προσβάλλων θρώσκει αὐτὸν αἰσθητικῶς καὶ μᾶλλον ἐπὶ τὰς ἀνομίας αὐτὸν ὁπλίζει, ἵνα τύχῃ πλείονος τιμωρίας, καὶ οὐ παύεται ἐπ᾽ ὀρέξεις ἁπλέτους τὴν ἐπιθυμίαν ἔχων, ἀκορέστως σκοτομαχῶν, καὶ τοῦ τον βασανίζει, καὶ ἐπ᾽ αὐτὸν πῦρ ἐπὶ τὸ πλεῖον αὐξάνει

> "I keep myself distant from the unreasonable, the rotten, the malicious, the jealous, the greedy, the bloodthirsty, the hubriatic, instead, giving them up to the avenging daemon, who assigns to them the sharpness of fire, who visibly assails them, and who equips them for more lawlessness so that they happen upon even more vengeance. For they cannot control their excessive yearnings, are always in the darkness - which tests them - and thus increase that fire even more."
> [1]

Which is basically the same understanding that Aeschylus revealed in his Oresteia trilogy many centuries before: the wisdom of pathei-mathos and the numinous pagan allegory of Μοῖραι τρίμορφοι μνήμονές τ᾽ Ἐρινύες [2], and which wisdom was also described by Milton over a millennia later by means of another allegory:

> The infernal Serpent; he it was, whose guile,
> Stirred up with envy and revenge, deceived
> The mother of mankind.

David Myatt
2015

∘∘∘

[1] *Poemandres*, 23. Corpus Hermeticum. Translated by David Myatt in *Poemandres, A Translation and Commentary*. 2014.

[2] Aeschylus (attributed), Prometheus Bound, 515-6

> τίς οὖν ἀνάγκης ἐστὶν οἰακοστρόφος.
> Μοῖραι τρίμορφοι μνήμονές τ' Ἐρινύες
>
> Who then compels to steer us?
> Trimorphed Moirai with their ever-heedful Furies

**Musings On Suffering, Human Nature,
And The Culture of Pathei-Mathos**

Part I

In respect of the question whether I am optimistic about our future as a species, I vacillate between optimism and pessimism, knowing from experience that the world contains people who do good things [1], people who do bad things, and people who when influenced or led or swayed by some-thing or someone can veer either way; and given that it seems as if in each generation there are those – many – who have not learned or who cannot learn from the pathei-mathos of previous generations, from the collective human πάθει μάθος – a culture of pathei-mathos thousands of years old – which reveals to us the beauty, the numinosity, of personal love, humility, and compassion, and the tragic lamentable unnecessary suffering caused by hubris, dishonour, selfishness, inconsiderance, intolerance, prejudice, hatred, war, extremism, and ideologies [2]. A world-wide suffering so evident, today, for example in the treatment of and the violence (by men) toward women; in the continuing armed conflicts – regional and local, over some-thing – that displace tens of thousands of people and cause destruction, injury, and hundreds of thousands of deaths; and in the killing of innocent people [3] by those who adhere to a harsh interpretation of some religion or some political ideology.

Do good people, world-wide, outweigh bad ones? My experiences and travels incline me to believe they do, although it seems as if the damage the bad ones do, the suffering they cause, sometimes and for a while outweighs the good that others do. But does the good done, in societies world-wide, now outweigh the bad done, especially such large-scale suffering as is caused by despots, corruption, armed conflict, and repressive regimes? Probably, at least in some societies. And yet even in such societies where, for example, education is widespread, there always seem to be selfish, dishonourable, inconsiderate, people; and also people such as the extremist I was with my hubriatic certitude-of-knowing inciting or causing hatred and violence and intolerance and glorifying war and kampf and trying to justify killing in the name of some abstraction or some belief or some cause or some ideology. People mostly, it seems, immune to and/or intolerant of the learning of the culture of pathei-mathos; a learning available to us in literature, music, Art, memoirs, in the aural and written recollections of those who endured or who witnessed hatred, violence, intolerance, conflict, war, and killing, and a learning also available in the spiritual message of those who taught humility, goodness, love, and tolerance. Immune or intolerant people who apparently can only change – or who could only possibly change for the better – only when they themselves are afflicted by such vicissitudes, such personal misfortune and suffering, as is the genesis of their own pathei-mathos.

Thus, and for example, in Europe there is a specific pathei-mathos that the years before the Second World War, and especially that war, wrought. A collective learning regarding intolerance, persecution, repression, hatred, injustice; a collective learning regarding the mass and the deliberate slaughter of people on account of their perceived or believed difference; and a learning, by a new generation, of the destruction, the suffering, the brutality, the horror, of a war where wrakeful machines and mass manufactured weapons played a significant role. Yet this specific pathei-mathos, containing the traumatic experiences of millions of people and forming as it now does an important part of the culture of pathei-mathos, has not prevented a resurgence in Europe of intolerance, prejudice, and a hatred based on perceived or believed difference; as witness my own doleful and suffering-causing decades of supporting and propagating the intolerance, the prejudice, the hatred, the violence, implicit in National-Socialism, and as witness the tens of thousands of others – perhaps the hundreds of thousands – in Europe who now support political organizations and movements which, while they are not overtly or even covertly National-Socialist, nevertheless seem to me to represent and propagate and encourage intolerance, and prejudice, and often the same type of hatred based on a perceived or a believed difference, be this difference a perceived ethnicity or a 'foreign religion' or a 'foreign culture' or a love for someone of the same gender. For it really seems as if the founders, the members, and the supporters, of such organizations and movements are, as I was for decades, immune to and/or intolerant of the learning that the culture of pathei-mathos makes accessible.

All this, while sad, is perhaps the result of our basic human nature; for we are jumelle, and not only because we are "deathful of body yet deathless the inner mortal" [4] but also because it seems to me that what is good and bad resides in us all [5], nascent or alive or as part of our personal past, and that it is just so easy, so tempting, so enjoyable, sometimes, to indulge in, to do, what is bad, and often harder for us to do what is right. Furthermore, we do seem to have a tendency – or perhaps a need – to ascribe what is bad to being 'out there', in something abstract or in others while neglecting or not perceiving our own faults and mistakes and while asserting or believing that we, and those similar to us or who we are in agreement with, are right and thus have the 'correct', the righteous, answers. Thus it is often easier to find what is bad 'out there' rather than within ourselves; easier to hate than to love, especially as a hatred of impersonal others sometimes affords us a reassuring sense of identity and a sense of being 'better' than those others.

Will it therefore require another thousand, or two thousand, or three thousand years – or more or less millennia – before we human beings en masse, world-wide, are empathic, tolerant, kind, and honourable? Is such a basic change in our nature even possible? Certainly there are some – and not only ideologues of one kind or another – who would argue and who have argued that such a change is not desirable. And is such a change in our nature contingent, as I incline to believe, upon the fair allocation of world resources and solving problems such as hunger and poverty and preventing preventable diseases? Furthermore, how can or could or should such a basic change be brought about – through an organized religion or religions, or through individual governments and their laws and their social and political and economic and educational policies, or through a collocation of governments, world-wide; or through individuals reforming themselves and personally educating others by means of, for example, the common culture of pathei-mathos which all humans share and which all human societies have contributed to for thousands of years? Which leads us on to questions regarding dogma, faith, and dissent; and to questions regarding government and compulsion and 'crime and punishment' and whether or not 'the needs of the many outweigh the needs of the few'; and also to questions regarding the efficacy of the reforming, spiritual, personal way given that spiritual ways teaching love, tolerance, humility, and compassion – and virtuous as they are, and alleviating and preventing suffering as they surely have – have not after several thousand years effected such a change in humans en masse.

I have to admit that I have no definitive or satisfactory answers to all these, and similar, questions; although my own pathei-mathos – and my lamentable four-decade long experience as an extremist, an ideologue, and as a selfish opinionated inconsiderate person – incline me to prefer the reforming, spiritual, personal way since I feel that such an approach, involving as it does a personal study of, a personal transmission of, the culture of pathei-mathos – and a personal knowing and a living of the humility that the culture of pathei-mathos teaches – is a way that does not cause nor contribute to the suffering that still so blights this world. A personal preference for such a numinous way even though I am aware of three things: of my past propensity to be wrong and thus of the necessary fallible nature of my answers; of the limited nature and thus the long time-scale (of many millennia) that such a way implies; and that it is possible, albeit improbable except in Science Fiction, that good people of honourable intentions may some day find a non-suffering-causing way by which governments or society or perhaps some new form of governance may in some manner bring about that change, en masse, in our human nature required to evolve us into individuals of empathy, compassion, and honour, who thus have something akin to a 'prime directive' to guide them in their dealings with those who are different, in whatever way, from ourselves.

Part II

Were I to daydream about some future time when such a galactic 'prime directive' exists, directing we spacefaring humans not to interfere in the internal affairs of non-terrans who are different, in whatever way, from ourselves, then I would be inclined to speculate that unless we by then have fundamentally and irretrievably changed ourselves for the better then it would not be long before some human or some human authority, somewhere, manufactured some sly excuse to order to try and justify ignoring it. For that is what we have done, among ourselves, for thousands of years; making then breaking some treaty or other; making some excuse to plunder resources; having some legal institution change some existing law or make some new law to give us the 'right' to do what it is we want to do; or manufacture some new legislative or governing body in order to 'legalize' what we do or have already done. Always using a plethora of words – and, latterly, legalese – to persuade others, and often ourselves, that what we do or are about to do or have already done is justified, justifiable, necessary, or right.

Perhaps the future excuse to so interfere contrary to a prime directive would be the familiar one of 'our security'; perhaps it would be an economic one of needing to exploit 'their' resources; perhaps it would be one regarding the threat of 'terrorism'; perhaps it would be the ancient human one, hallowed by so much blood, of 'our' assumed superiority, of 'their system' being 'repressive' or 'undemocratic' or of they – those 'others' – being 'backward' or 'uncivilized' and in need of being enlightened and 're-educated' by our 'progressive' ideas. Or, more probable, it would be some new standard or some new fashionable political or social or even religious dogma by which we commend ourselves on our progress and which we use, consciously or otherwise, to judge others by.

The current reality is that even if we had or soon established a terran 'prime directive' directing we humans not to interfere in the internal affairs of other humans here on Earth who are different, in whatever way, from ourselves, it is fairly certain it "would not be long before some human or some human authority, somewhere, manufactured some sly excuse to order to try and justify ignoring it..."

Which mention of a terran 'prime directive' leads to two of the other questions which cause me to vacillate between optimism and pessimism in regard to our future as a species. The question of increasing population, and the question of the finite resources of this Earth. Which suggests to me, as some others, that – especially as the majority of people now live in urban areas – a noble option is for us, as a species, to cooperate and betake ourselves to colonize our Moon, then Mars, and seek to develop such technology as would take us beyond our Solar System. For if we do not do this then the result would most probably be, at some future time, increasing conflict over land and resources, mass migrations (probably resulting in more conflict) and such governments or authorities as then exist forced by economic circumstance to adopt policies to reduce or limit their own population. Global problems probably exasperated still further by the detrimental changes that available evidence indicates could possibly result from what has been termed 'climate change' [6].

But is the beginning of this noble option of space colonization viable in the near future? Possibly not, given that a country such as America, for instance, while having the resources and the space expertise and the technology necessary – and the means to develop existing space technology – currently (2013) allocates only 0.5% of its federal budget to NASA while allocating over 20% to military expenditure [7].

Which leads we human beings, with our jumelle character, confined to this small planet we call Earth, possibly continuing as we have, for millennia, continued: a quarrelsome species, often engaged (like primates) in minor territorial disputes; in our majority unempathic; often inconsiderate, often prejudiced (even though we like to believe otherwise); often inclined to place our self-interest and our pleasure first; often prone to being manipulated or to manipulating others; often addicted to the slyness of words spoken and written and heard and read; often believing 'we' are better than 'them'; and fighting, raping, hating, killing, invading here, interfering there. And beset by the problems wrought by increasing population, by dwindling resources, by mass migrations, by continuing armed conflicts (regional, local, supranational, over some-thing) and possibly also affected by the effects of climate change.

Yet also, sometimes despite ourselves, we are beings capable of – and have shown over millennia – compassion, kindness, gentleness, tolerance, love, fairness, reason, and a valourous self-sacrifice that is and has been inspirational. But perhaps above all we have, in our majority, exuded and kept and replenished the virtue of hope; hoping, dreaming, of better times, a better future, sometime, somewhere – and not, as it happens, for ourselves but for our children and their children and the future generations yet to be born. And it is this hope that changes us, and has changed us, for the better, as our human culture of pathei-mathos so eloquently, so numinously, and so tragically, reveals.

Thus the question seems to be whether we still have hope enough, dreams enough, nobility enough, and can find some way to change ourselves, to thus bring a better – a more fairer, more just, more compassionate – future into-being without causing or contributing to the suffering which so blights, and which has so blighted, our existence on Earth.

Personally, I am inclined to believe that the way we need, the hope, the dream, we need is that of setting forth to colonize our Moon, then Mars, and then the worlds beyond our Solar System, guided by a prime directive.

David Myatt
2013

Notes

[1] I understand 'the good' as what alleviates or does not cause suffering; what is compassionate; what is honourable; what is reasoned and balanced. Honour being here, and elsewhere in my recent writings, understood as the instinct for and an adherence to what is fair, dignified, and valourous.

[2] I have expanded, a little, on what I mean by 'the culture of pathei-mathos' in my tract *Questions of Good, Evil, Honour, and God*.

[3] As defined by my 'philosophy of pathei-mathos', I understand innocence as "an attribute of those who, being personally unknown to us, are therefore unjudged us by and who thus are given the benefit of the doubt. For this presumption of innocence of others – until direct personal experience, and individual and empathic knowing of them, prove otherwise – is the fair, the reasoned, the numinous, the human, thing to do. Empathy and πάθει μάθος incline us toward treating other human beings as we ourselves would wish to be treated; that is they incline us toward fairness, toward self-restraint, toward being well-mannered, and toward an appreciation and understanding of innocence."

[4] Pœmandres (Corpus Hermeticum), 15 – διὰ τοῦτο παρὰ πάντα τὰ ἐπὶ γῆς ζῷα διπλοῦς ἐστιν ὁ ἄνθρωπος

As I noted in my translation of and commentary on the Pœmandres tract, "Jumelle. For διπλοῦς. The much underused and descriptive English word jumelle – from the Latin gemellus – describes some-thing made in, or composed of, two parts, and is therefore most suitable here, more so than common words such as 'double' or twofold."

[5] qv. Sophocles, Antigone, v.334, vv.365-366

> πολλὰ τὰ δεινὰ κοὐδὲν ἀνθρώπου δεινότερον πέλει...
> σοφόν τι τὸ μηχανόεν τέχνας ὑπὲρ ἐλπίδ᾽ ἔχων
> τοτὲ μὲν κακόν, ἄλλοτ᾽ ἐπ᾽ ἐσθλὸν ἕρπει

> There exists much that is strange, yet nothing
> Has more strangeness than a human being...
> Beyond his own hopes, his cunning
> In inventive arts – he who arrives
> Now with dishonour, then with chivalry

[6] Many people have a view about 'climate change' – for or against – for a variety of reasons. My own view is that the scientific evidence available at the moment seems to indicate that there is a change resulting from human activity and that this change could possibility be detrimental, in certain ways, to us and to the other life with which we share this planet. The expressions 'seems to indicate' and 'could possibly be' are necessary given that this view of mine might need to be, and should be, reassessed if and when new evidence or facts become available.

Also, there remains the possibility that some or even most of this climate change may be caused, or has in the past been caused, by extra-terrestrial factors we currently do not fully understand, such as the natural movement, the journey, of our solar system through the spiral arms of our galaxy [qv, for instance, Filipović, Horner, Crawford, Tothill. Mass Extinction And The Structure Of The Milky Way, Serbian Astronomical Journal. September 2013].

[7] According to figures in the Fiscal Year 2014 Budget of the U.S. Government, the maximum ever allocated to NASA was 4%, during the Apollo programme.

Blue Reflected Starlight

As it departed toward the vastness of interstellar space, the Voyager 1 interplanetary spacecraft in 1990(ce) transmitted an image of Earth from a distance of over four billion miles; the most distant image of Earth we human beings have ever seen. The Earth, our home, was a bluish dot; a mere Cosmic speck among the indefinity, visible only because of reflected starlight and - in the solar panorama imaged by Voyager on that February day - of no observed importance. One speck in one galaxy in a vast Cosmos of billions upon billions of galaxies, and one speck that would most probably appear, to a non-terran, less interesting than the rings of Saturn, just visible from such a distance.

Yet we human beings, en masse, continue to live in a manner which not only belies our Cosmic insignificance but which militates against the empathy, the humility, that such a Cosmic perspective can and does engender. Thus do we individually, as well as collectively, have pride in our lives, our deeds, our 'accomplishments', just as we continue to exploit not only other human beings but the Earth itself: and exploit for pleasure, or profit, or from some desire or because of some cause or some faith or some ideology or some ideation we believe in or support. Either believing or asserting, in our hubris, that we 'know'

- that we 'understand' - what we are doing, or reckless of consequences because unable or unwilling to control our desires; unable or unwilling to control ourselves or our addiction to some cause or some faith or some ideology or some ideation.

Thus does the suffering we here inflict on other life - human and otherwise - continue. Thus does our human-wrought destruction continue, as if we are in thrall consciously or otherwise to the ideation that our planet, and its life including other humans, are some kind of 'resource', a means to supply our needs or a way to satiate our desires. So easy, so very easy, to injure, hate, and kill. So easy, so very easy, to satiate the desire to be in control. So very easy to place ourselves first; even easier to have our feelings, our desires, subsume, overcome, whatever consideration we might give, or previously had given, to others and to other life. So easy, so very easy, to make excuses - consciously or otherwise - to ourselves, and to others, for what we have done or what we are about to do; for always there is the excuse of self-interest or self-preservation, or the excuse of desires or some cause or some faith or some ideology or some ideation. So easy, so very easy, to spew forth words.

It is as if we terrans, en masse, have forgotten, keep forgetting, or have never discovered the wisdom that what involves too many words - and especially what involves or requires speeches, rhetoric, propaganda, dogma - is what obscures empathy and thus the numinosity that empathy reveals; the numinosity presented to us by the pathei-mathos of our human past; manifest to us - and living now - in the way of living of those whose personal pathei-mathos - whose personal experience of suffering, death, destruction, hate, violence, of too many killings - has forever changed them. The numinous revelation of kindness, of humility, of gentleness, of love, of compassion; of being able to restrain, control, ourselves; of being able to comprehend our small, insignificant, place in the indefinity of the Cosmos, bringing as this comprehension does an understanding of the importance, the numinosity, that is a shared and loyal love between two people: and revealing as this does the Cosmic unimportance of such wars and conflicts and such brutality as have blighted our terran history.

As I know from my outré experience of life - especially my forty years of extremism, hubris, and selfishness; my terms of imprisonment, my experience with gangs, with people of bad intentions and with those of good intentions - it really is as if we terran men have, en masse, learnt nothing from the past four or five thousand years. For the uncomfortable truth is that we, we men, are and have been the ones causing, needing, participating in, those wars and conflicts. We - not women - are the cause of most of the suffering, death, destruction, hate, violence, brutality, and killing, that has occurred and which is still occurring, thousand year upon thousand year; just as we are the ones who seek to be - or who often need to be - prideful and 'in control'; and the ones who through greed or alleged need or because of some ideation have saught to exploit not only other human beings but the Earth itself. We are also masters of deception; of the lie. Cunning with our excuses, cunning in persuasion, and skilled at inciting hatred and violence. And yet we men have also shown ourselves to be, over thousands of years, valourous; capable of noble, selfless, deeds. Capable of doing what is fair and restraining ourselves from doing what is unethical. Capable of a great and a gentle love.

This paradoxy continues to perplex me. And I have no answers as to how we might change, reform, this paradoxical φύσις of ours, and so - perhaps - balance the suffering-causing masculous with the empathic muliebral and yet somehow in some way retain that which is the genesis of the valourous. And if we cannot do this, if we cannot somehow reform ourselves, can we terrans as a species survive, and do we deserve to?

Are we, we men here on this planet, capable of restraining and reforming ourselves, en masse, such that we allow ourselves, and are given, no excuses of whatever kind from whatever source for our thousand year upon thousand year of violence against women? Are we capable of such a reformation of our kind that such reprehensible violence against women by cowardly men becomes only historical fact?

Are we, here on this planet, capable of restraining and reforming ourselves, en masse, such that we allow ourselves no excuses of whatever kind from whatever source for wars, armed conflicts, brutality against perceived or stated 'enemies', and murderous intervention? Such a reformation of ourselves that wars, armed conflicts, such brutality, and such interventions, become only historical fact?

Or are we fated, under Sun, to squabble and bicker and hate and kill and destroy and exploit this planet and its life until we, a failed species, leave only dead detritic traces of our hubris?

Or will we, or some of us, betake ourselves away to colonize faraway non-terran places, taking with us our unreformed paradoxical φύσις to perchance again despoil, destroy, as some of our kind once betook themselves away to forever change parts of this speck of blue reflected starlight which gave us this fortunity of Life?

Yet again I admit I have no answers.

David Myatt
2012

The above text is part of a letter, sent in November 2012, to a personal correspondent in response to her reply to an earlier letter of mine, part of which earlier letter - titled *A Slowful Learning, Perhaps* - is included below.

A Slowful Learning, Perhaps

"And what the dead had no speech for, when living,
They can tell you, being dead: the communication
Of the dead is tongued with fire beyond the language of the living." [1]

Perhaps it is incumbent upon us to now celebrate, remember, transcribe, only the kind, the gentle, the loving, the compassionate, the happy, and the personal, things - and those who have done them - and not the many things that have caused suffering, death, destruction, and inflicted violence on others. For, so often it seems, we human beings have and have had for millennia a somewhat barbaric propensity to celebrate, to remember, to transcribe, our seeming triumphs of personal pride and of victory over others - be such others some declared enemy or some designated foe - always or almost always forgetting the suffering, the deaths, the destruction, that such a seeming, and always transient, victory over others has always involved, and always or almost always forgetting the suffering, the hurt, the unhappiness, that our selfish prideful desire to triumph, to succeed, causes in someone or some many somewhere.

For millennia so many have been fixated on either our selves - our pride, our success, our needs, our desires - or on the pride, the success, the needs, the security, the prosperity, we have assigned to or we accepted as a necessary part of some ideal, some entity, some supra-personal abstraction.

Thus, anciently, in the name of some Pharaoh or some Caesar, or some King, or some Chief, or some leader, or some religious faith, or on behalf of some interpretation of some religious faith, we sallied forth to war or to battle, causing suffering, death, destruction, and doing violence, to others. Invading here; invading there. Attacking here; interfering there. Defending this, or defending that. Destroying this, or destroying that.

Thus, latterly, in the name of some country, or some nation, or some political ideal, or some cause, or on behalf of some-thing supra-personal we believed in, we sallied for to war or did deeds that caused suffering, death, destruction, and inflicted violence on others. Defending this, or attacking that. Invading here; or colonizing there. Dreaming of or determined to find glory. Always, always, using the excuse that our cause, our ideal, our country, our nation, our security, our prosperity, our 'way of life', our 'destiny', hallowed our deeds; believing that such suffering, death, destruction as we caused, and the violence we inflicted on others, were somehow justified because 'we' were right and 'they' our foes, were wrong or in some way not as 'civilized' or as 'just' as us since 'their cause' or their 'way of life' or way of doing things was, according to us, reprehensible.

Whose voice now tells the story of all or even most of those who suffered and those who died in conflicts four thousand years ago? Three thousand, two thousand, years ago?

It is as if we, as a sentient species, have learnt nothing from the past four thousand years. Nothing from the accumulated pathei-mathos of those who did such deeds or who experienced such deeds or who suffered because of such deeds. Learnt nothing from four thousand years of the human culture that such pathei-mathos created and which to us is manifest - remembered, celebrated, transcribed - in Art, literature, memoirs, music, poetry, myths, legends, and often in the ethos of a numinous ancestral awareness or in those sometimes mystical allegories that formed the basis for a spiritual way of life.

All we have done is to either (i) change the names of that which or those whom we are loyal to and for which or for whom we fight, kill, and are prepared to die for, or (ii) given names to such new causes as we have invented in order to give us some identity or some excuse to fight, endure, triumph, preen, or die for. Pharaoh, Caesar, Pope, Defender of the Faith, President, General, Prime Minister; Rome, Motherland, Fatherland, The British Empire, Our Great Nation, North, South, our democratic way of life. It makes little difference; the same loyalty; the same swaggering; the same hubris; the same desire, or the same obligation or coercion, to participate and fight.

How many human beings, for instance, have been killed in the last hundred years in wars and conflicts? Wars and conflicts hallowed, or justified, by someone or some many somewhere. One hundred million dead? More? How many more hundreds of millions have suffered because of such modern wars and conflicts?

It is almost as if we - somehow flawed - need something beyond our personal lives to vivify us; to excite us; to test ourselves; to identify with. As if we cannot escape the barbarian who lies in wait, within; ready to subsume us once again so that we sally forth on behalf of some cause, some leader, or some ideal, or some abstraction, or as part of some crusade. As if we human beings, as Sophocles intimated over two thousand years ago, are indeed, by nature, and have remained sometimes honourable and sometimes dishonourable beings [2], able to sometimes be rational, thinking, beings, but also unable to escape our desire, our need, our propensity, to not only be barbaric but to try to justify to ourselves and to others our need for, and even our enjoyment of, such barbarity.

Or perhaps the stark truth is that it is we men who are flawed or incomplete and who thus need to change. As if we, we men, have not yet evolved enough to be able to temper, to balance, our harsh masculous nature with the muliebral; a balance which would see us become almost a new species; one which has, having finally sloughed off the suffering-causing hubriatic patriarchal attitudes of the past, learnt from the pathei-mathos of our ancestors, from the pathei-mathos of our human culture, born and grown and nurtured as our human culture was, has been, and is by over four thousand years of human-caused suffering. A learning from and of the muliebral, for the wyrdful thread which runs through, which binds, our human pathei-mathos is a muliebral one: the thread of kindness, of gentleness, of love, of compassion; of empathy; of the personal over and above the supra-personal.

A learning that reveals to us a quite simple truth; that what is wrong is causing or contributing to suffering, and that, with (at least in my admittedly fallible opinion) one exception and one exception only [3] we cannot now (again, at least in my admittedly fallible opinion) morally justify intentionally causing or contributing to the suffering of any living being.

How many more centuries - or millennia - will we need? To learn, to change, to cease to cause such suffering as we have for so many millennia caused.

My own life - of four decades of suffering-causing extremism and personal selfishness - is, most certainly, just one more example of our manful capacity to be stupid and hubriatic. To fail to learn from the pathei-mathos of human culture, even though I personally had the advantages of a living in diverse cultures and of a 'classical education', and thus was taught or became familiar with the insights of Lao Tzu, of Siddhartha Gautama, of Jesus of Nazareth, of Sappho, Sophocles, Aeschylus, Cicero, Livy, Marcus Aurelius, Dante Alighieri, Jane Austen, Charles Dickens, TS Eliot, EM Forster, and so many others; and even though I had the opportunity to discover, to participate in, and thus felt, the numinosity, the learning, inherent in so many other things, from plainchant to Byrd, Dowland, Palestrina, Tallis, to JS Bach and beyond. And yet, despite all these advantages, all these chances to learn, to evolve, I remained hubriatic; selfish, arrogant, in thrall to ideations, and like so many men somewhat addicted to the joy, to the pleasures, of kampf, placing pursuit of that pleasure, or some cause, or some ideation, or my own needs, before loved ones, family, friends. Only learning, only finally and personally learning, after a death too far.

Is that then to be our human tragedy? That most of us cannot or will not learn - that we cannot change - until we, personally, have suffered enough or have encountered, or experienced, or caused, one death too many?

David Myatt
November 2012

Notes

[1] TS Eliot, *Little Gidding*

[2] As Sophocles expressed it:

πολλὰ τὰ δεινὰ κοὐδὲν ἀνθρώπου δεινότερον πέλει...

σοφόν τι τὸ μηχανόεν τέχνας ὑπὲρ ἐλπίδ᾽ ἔχων
τοτὲ μὲν κακόν, ἄλλοτ᾽ ἐπ᾽ ἐσθλὸν ἕρπει

There exists much that is strange, yet nothing
Has more strangeness than a human being...
Beyond his own hopes, his cunning
In inventive arts – he who arrives
Now with dishonour, then with chivalry

Antigone, v.334, vv.365-366

[3] The one exception is personal honour; the valourous use of force in a personal situation. As mentioned in *The Way of Pathei-Mathos - A Philosophical Compendiary*:

" [The] balancing of compassion – of the need not to cause suffering – by σωφρονεῖν and δίκη is perhaps most obvious on that particular occasion when it may be judged necessary to cause suffering to another human being. That is, in honourable self-defence. For it is natural – part of our reasoned, fair, just, human nature – to defend ourselves when attacked and (in the immediacy of the personal moment) to valorously, with chivalry, act in defence of someone close-by who is unfairly attacked or dishonourably threatened or is being bullied by others, and to thus employ, if our personal judgement of the circumstances deem it necessary, lethal force.

This use of force is, importantly, crucially, restricted – by the individual nature of our judgement, and by the individual nature of our authority – to such personal situations of immediate self-defence and of valorous defence of others, and cannot be extended beyond that, for to so extend it, or attempt to extend it beyond the immediacy of the personal moment of an existing physical threat, is an arrogant presumption – an act of ὕβρις – which negates the fair, the human, presumption of innocence of those we do not personally know, we have no empathic knowledge of, and who present no direct, immediate, personal, threat to us or to others nearby us.

Such personal self-defence and such valorous defence of another in a personal situation are in effect a means to restore the natural balance which the unfair, the dishonourable, behaviour of others upsets. That is, such defence fairly, justly, and naturally in the immediacy of the moment corrects their error of ὕβρις resulting from their bad (their rotten) φύσις; a rotten character evident in their lack of the virtue, the skill, of σωφρονεῖν. For had they possessed that virtue, and if their character was not bad, they would not have undertaken such a dishonourable attack."

Toward Humility - A Brief Personal View

The more I reflect on religion – and on my experience of various religions and those who believe in them – the more I incline toward the view that most if not all of what have sometimes been referred to as 'the major religions' – Christianity, Islam, Judaism, Hinduism, Sikhism – manifest (each in their own particular way) and enhance (or can enhance) our humanity, and thus enshrine a means for us to be compassionate and tolerant and receptive to humility. For it seems to me there is, to paraphrase an expression of George Fox used by The Religious Society of Friends, 'that of the numinous' in every person, and that answering to 'that of the numinous' can and has taken various manifestations over millennia with all such manifestations deserving of respect since there is an underlying unity, a similar spiritual essence – a similar discovery and knowing and appreciation of the numinous, a similar understanding of the error of hubris – beyond those different outer manifestations and the different terms and expressions and allegories used to elucidate 'that of the numinous'.

Thus it would be improper and erroneous of me to conclude that a particular religion has influenced more people in a good way – is 'better' – than another religion or all other religions. Especially as – and again in my admittedly fallible view – the bad done, the suffering caused, by those 'in the name of' some religion or by adherents of some religion, most probably are caused by or are a consequence of our errors, our faults, our propensity as human beings to be hubriatic, to sometimes or often do or sanction what is dishonourable, inhuman, or just plain selfish.

As for Buddhism, I tend to view it – like Taoism – as a Way of Life rather than as a religion [2] and even if considered a religion then most probably it is a noble exception considering how, unlike many religions, it has seldom if ever been associated with people and tyrants who followed it doing dishonourable, inhuman, extremist, deeds in its name. Certainly Buddhism – and Taoism and many others Ways – have not (so far as I know) been used by fallible hubriatic humans to try to justify wars, invasions, persecution, killing, intolerance, and the mistreatment of those deemed to be heretics and apostates.

The discovery and knowing and thus the appreciation of the numinous by individuals, in a life-changing and thus often reformatory way, is frequently the result of pathei-mathos, and which pathei-mathos can incline individuals toward their own uncertitude of knowing and thus toward a certain personal humility. A personal humility which I personally believe manifests – which is – the essence of the numinous and thus the essence of our humanity, of our nature as human beings capable of reason, compassion, love, honour, and gentleness; human beings who have the ability to choose not to commit the error of hubris; the ability not to do what is harsh, dishonourable, hateful, violent; the ability to refrain from inflicting suffering on other humans and other living beings; the ability to be empathic and thus appreciate the connexion we are to all Life, to ψυχή.

In my own case, as I mentioned in *Just My Fallible Views, Again*:

> "Being with – living with – Muslims (both Sunni and Shia) taught me humility [3], the ignorance of my past political beliefs, and how the Muslim way of life can be and certainly has been (on balance) an influence for good, just as Christianity (on balance) is and has been, and just as Judaism is and has been [...]
>
> Hence I find myself in the curious position of now possibly understanding and appreciating the wordless raison d'etat of Catholic monasticism, manifest as this is in a personal humility; a humility that during my time as a monk my then still hubriatic self could not endure for long. Which recent understanding and appreciation led me for a short while at least, and only a few years ago, to wistfully if unrealistically yearn to return to that particular secluded way of life. And unrealistic because for all that understanding, appreciation, and yearning, I no longer had the type of faith that was required, the type of Christian faith I did have when I had lived that monastic way of life. A lack of faith I really discovered and felt when I went, during that not-too-long-ago period of yearning, to stay once again and for a while in a monastery [...]
>
> Also, although I no longer consider myself a Muslim, I retain a great respect for that particular Way of Life, as I do for several other Ways I have personal experience of, such as Christianity, Buddhism, and Taoism. And a respect for two basic reasons. First, because I feel that those (and many other Ways and religions, for example Judaism and Hinduism) have been and are a means to remind us of the numinous, of the error of hubris, of the need for a certain personal humility. For they all, diverse as they appear to be, can enable us to glimpse or feel or know that supra-personal perspective which inclines us or can incline us toward living a more moral life, expressed as such a life often is in personal virtues such as compassion, self-restraint, honesty, modesty. Second, because I am acutely aware of how fallible I am, that I could be wrong, that I have been wrong in the past, and that my answers to certain philosophical, theological, and moral questions (as evident for example in my philosophy of pathei-mathos) are only my own often tentative and certainly fallible answers."

For me personally, humility is also an acknowledgement of a particular and important intuition regarding the self, regarding our perception of ourselves. Of how – when as individuals via pathei-mathos or otherwise we experience and then appreciate the numinous – we are not (as we often like to believe) in control of our lives, but instead are subject to supra-personal forces that have often, in the past as now, been variously termed or described as God, the gods, Fate, karma, Allah, wyrd, the cosmic perspective, the acausal, destiny, Μοῖραι τρίμορφοι μνήμονές τ᾽ Ἐρινύες, and so on. Of how such a belief of personally being in control, or of being capable of so being in control, of our lives, is mere egoism at best and, at worst, hubris; an egoism and a hubris that, whether we know or not – and mostly we with our egoism and our hubris do not know – are both the genesis of suffering and the raison d'etat behind our perpetuation of suffering.

David Myatt
September 2012

Notes

[1] Humility is used here, in a spiritual context, to refer to that gentleness, that modest demeanour, that understanding, which derives from an appreciation of the numinous and also from one's own admitted uncertainty of knowing and one's acknowledgement of past mistakes. An uncertainty of knowing, an acknowledgement of mistakes, that often derive from πάθει μάθος.

Humility is thus the natural human balance that offsets the unbalance of hubris (ὕβρις) – the balance that offsets the unbalance of pride and arrogance, and the balance that offsets the unbalance of that certainty of knowing which is one basis for extremism, for extremist beliefs, for fanaticism and intolerance. That is, humility is a manifestation of the natural balance of Life; a restoration of ἁρμονίη, of δίκη, of σωφρονεῖν – of those qualities and virtues – that hubris and extremism, that ἔρις and πόλεμος, undermine, distance us from, and replace.

[2] My experience of various religions – and of other elucidations of 'that of the numinous' – has led me to conclude that it is possible to make a distinction between a religion and a Way of Life. One of the differences being that a religion requires and manifests a codified ritual and doctrine and a certain expectation of conformity in terms of doctrine and ritual, as well as a certain organization beyond the local community level resulting in particular individuals assuming or being appointed to positions of authority in matters relating to that religion. In contrast, Ways are more diverse and more an expression of a spiritual ethos, of a customary, and often localized, way of doing certain spiritual things, with there generally being little or no organization beyond the community level and no individuals assuming – or being appointed by some organization – to positions of authority in matters relating to that ethos.

Religions thus tend to develope an organized regulatory and supra-local hierarchy which oversees and appoints those, such as priests or religious teachers, regarded as proficient in spiritual matters and in matters of doctrine and ritual, whereas adherents of Ways tend to locally and informally and communally, and out of respect and a personal knowing, accept certain individuals as having a detailed knowledge and an understanding of the ethos and the practices of that Way.

[3] In terms of my own pathei-mathos, the culture of Islam – manifest in Adab, in Namaz, and in a reliance on only Allah, and a culture lived, experienced, by me over a period of some nine years – was not only a new revelation of the numinous but also a grounding in practical humility. The very performance of Namaz requires and cultivates an attitude of personal humility, most obvious in Sajdah, the prostration to and in the presence of Allah, Ar-Rahman, Ar-Raheem; a personal humility encouraged by Adab, and shared in Jummah Namaz in a Masjid and during Ramadan.

A Catholic Still, In Spirit?

Perhaps I remain, partially at least, a Catholic in spirit – in my heart – though not, most of the time, in words and deeds. For while I intellectually and empathically disagree with the teachings of the Catholic Church on many matters – such as homosexuality, contraception, and on divorcées who have remarried being excluded from Holy Communion (unless they have resorted to a Papal Annulment) – I still find myself in my inner weakness not only sometimes frequenting the Lady Chapel of my nearest RC Church – lighting a candle, kneeling, and in reverent silent contemplative prayer remembering, in the felt presence of The Blessed Virgin Mary, those now dead loved ones such as my mother and father and Sue and Francis, and those other women hurt by my selfishness – but also traveling several times a year to where Gregorian chant is sung and where the Tridentine Mass is celebrated, bringing as such Latin chant and such a Latin Mass still do, in me, a renewed awareness of the numinous and a renewal of such humility as I strive – and sometimes still so often fail – to remember and feel.

There seems to me no intricate and difficult interior problem here derived from my somewhat paganus way of pathei-mathos, for that way is essentially – for me, even born as it is from my own pathei-mathos – rather intellectual, a perceiveration, lacking as it does something outward, practical, supra-personal, and communal, to presence the numinous and thus affect one's very being in a spiritual way. So I seem to now exist – and have for several years existed – between two worlds: apparently emotionally needing something practical, living, and spiritual beyond myself and my intellectualism, and yet knowing in a rather unemotional manner that it is the way of pathei-mathos, and not Catholicism, which is my weltanschauung.

No intricate and difficult interior problem, no inner dichotomy, because I know the many flaws in my weltanschauung and in myself; and one cannot intellectually create some-thing – manufacture some-thing devoid of ψυχή – to presence the numinous. For it seems to me that such a presencing has to evolve, organically, over causal time, because it has been wordlessly presenced in other mortals and then kept alive because also felt by some of a newer generation. Will – can – such a presencing of the numinous arise from that way of pathei-mathos? Most probably not, intellectual and so very personal as it is.

So the need for some inner, numinous, sustenance remains; for fulfilling as a lot of classical music – such as the Cantatas of JS Bach – is and are, and fulfilling as walks alone in wild and rural Nature are, I sense a yearning in me for something more: some wordless intimation of the Divine which betakes me so far away from my still egoistic self that I am both awed and humbled again, as I often was in Winter wandering a darkened cloister as a monk in that quiet contemplative time between Matins and Lauds.

David Myatt
2015

Some Personal Perceiverations

Being, Death, Becoming

In the course of the past forty-five years or so of my adult life, I seem to have arrived at an unplanned destination so far removed and so different from where I started it is almost as if I have found not only another world but also another person. As if the I, the youthful self, who existed at the beginning of my journey, has vanished, died, to be mysteriously replaced by another being. For how did that young, that violent, that fanatical, that thuggish, that racist, neo-nazi become transformed into this aged man of the greying hair for whom the most important thing is a loyal love shared between two human beings and who now quietly, peacefully, preaches personal virtues such as empathy, gentleness, compassion, and εὐταξία, and who understands racism for the inhumanity it is?

No, it was not several terms of imprisonment for violence that led to the death of that egotistical arrogant self; nor even nearly two years as a Christian monk. Not even a year spent working in a hospital as a student nurse in those days, long-gone, when such training was mostly practical. Nor even being arrested on suspicion of conspiracy to murder with the prospect of years, possibly decades, in jail.

No, not that conversion to Islam and the almost eight years lived after that. Nor even the forthsithe of the first of two loved ones suddenly unexpectedly taken from me: her death no end then of that, my so selfish vainglorious self.

No, it was none of those, and similar things, in isolation. For that selfish self lived on. Slightly changed, but never changed enough. A self though increasingly divided and struggling within with certain moral dilemmas never divided enough, never struggling enough, since always always a fateful thread unwoven from abstractions began to bind, repair, restore.

For decades, no satori, no enlightenment, engulfed, overwhelmed. No one moment, no one defining event, to change, transform one forever as understanding suddenly dawned. Instead, it was the steady accumulation of experience; the accumulation of personal mistakes, of personal folly year following year, of moral dilemma following moral dilemma; a slow learning – a very slow learning – drip drip dripping away at my surety, my arrogance, my beliefs, as sea-water surging drips away at seemingly stronger rock.

No, no satori – until a second forthsithing came to shock, shake, betake, me; her death a potion to that self but six warm Summers ago. But even then, the poisoned dying self lingered on: three more Winters until a new Spring burst forth with healing Sun so that his dying finally became his death and brought forth a new individual replete, complete, with sorrow.

Sorrow and Love

Following the suicide of my fiancée in 2006, one of the first practical things I instinctively did – I was moved, felt almost compelled, to do – was travel to visit the nearest Catholic Church and, in remembrance of her, light a candle in the Lady Chapel before the statue of the Blessed Virgin Mary.

This instinctive heart-felt act following such a personal tragedy afterwards rather surprised me, an act perhaps brought forth by my upbringing as a Catholic and my time as a monk. Surprised me, for I was still then, nominally at least, a Muslim, and so in theory should have made dua to Allah or travelled to the nearest Mosque. Thus began an intense interior process of reflexion which was to last some three years, and which was to lead to me developing, refining, my philosophy of The Numinous Way and thus to turning away from the way of al-Islam, away from all causal abstractions.

Part of the personal understanding so developed was that, in respect of other spiritual ways, there was for me a tolerance, a respect; a knowing that my own answers are just my own fallible answers, and that, as I wrote last year:

> "...any Way or religion which manifests, which expresses, which guides individuals toward, the numinous humility we human beings need is good, and should not be stridently condemned. For such personal humility – that which prevents us from committing hubris, whatever the raison d'être, the theology, the philosophy – is a presencing of the numinous. Indeed, one might write and say that it is a personal humility – whatever the source – that expresses our true developed (that is, rational and empathic) human nature and which nature such Ways or religions or mythological allegories remind us

of." *Soli Deo Gloria*

Furthermore:

> Þeȝ sume men bo þurȝut gode,
> an þurȝut clene on hore mode,
> ho[m] longeþ honne noþeles.
> Þat boþ her, [w]o is hom þes:
> vor þeȝ hi bon hom solue iborȝe,
> hi ne soþ her nowiȝt bote sorwe.
> Vor oþer men hi wepeþ sore,
> an for hom biddeþ Cristes ore.

The Owl and The Nightingale, c. 1275 ce [1]

> Though some men be thoroughly good
> An thoroughly clean of heart
> How longeth they nonetheless
> They be not here
> For though their soul be saved
> They seeth nought but grieving here:
> For they for men's sorrows weep
> And for themself biddeth Christ have mercy

For there was, and remains, a deep sorrow within me; born from a knowing of inexcusable personal mistakes made, inexcusable suffering caused, of fortunities lost; a sorrow deepened by a knowing, a feeling, a learning, of how important, how human, a personal love is. Indeed, that love is the most important, the most human, the most numinous, virtue of all.

The Infortunity of Abstractions

The fateful sorrow-causing thread which ran through and which, for nearly four decades, bound and blighted my adult life is the thread of idealism born of the belief that in order to achieve some posited, imagined, 'ideal', generalized, and future, state of affairs, certain sacrifices have to made by people in the present 'for the greater good' – sacrifices of their happiness, their love, even of their lives. And not sacrifices for one's self, one's loved ones, one's family – but 'for the greater good', with this 'greater good' being described, championed, by politicians, by 'statesmen', by leaders, by 'representatives of the people', or even in former times by potentates, religious leaders, and military commanders.

A 'greater good' variously described and named. For many, it is their 'nation'; for others, 'patriotic/religious/political duty'; for others, it is 'their people' or their 'race'. For others still, it is called 'freedom', or 'democracy', or 'justice' or even, in former times, 'destiny' or God or 'Empire'. The names change, are even sometimes interchangeable, but the thread of love-destroying idealism remains.

Thus, in the name of such things one justifies the use of deadly force and violence so that one goes to war, or supports war; or supports violent revolution. One kills, or supports killing. In the name of such things one justifies a war, an invasion, a revolution, violence, the killing of 'the enemy'. All in the hope that the world of tomorrow will be better than the world of today. A hope alive, kept alive, while thousands, tens of thousands, hundreds of thousands, millions, of human beings are killed, injured, and suffer, century upon century, millennia after millennia.

For decades this idealism, this hope, such justification, that thread, gave life, vigour, to the selfish person I was: violent, inciting, propagandistic, fanatical, preacher of revolution, war. But now that thread has, wyrdfully, thankfully, been broken at the cost perhaps of a beautiful life, her death a constant painful reminder that, for me, such love-destroying idealism is:

> "...fundamentally wrong and inhuman. That is, it is a manufactured abstraction, a great cause of suffering, and that nothing – no idealism, no cause, no ideal, no dogma, no perceived duty – is worth or justifies the suffering of any living-being, sentient or otherwise. That it is empathy, compassion and a personal love which are human, the essence of our humanity: not some abstract notion of duty; not some idealism. That it is the impersonal interference in the affairs of others – based on some cause, some belief, some dogma, some perceived duty, some ideology, some creed, some ideal, some manufactured abstraction – which causes and greatly contributes to suffering, and which moves us far away from empathy and compassion and thus diverts us from our humanity and from changing ourselves, in a quiet way, into a more evolved, a more empathic and more compassionate, human being." *A Change of Perspective* (2010)

Now, all I – touched by sorrow – can do now is gently, quietly, reclusively, strive to capture, recapture, a little something of the world of love.

> The moment of sublime knowing
> As clouds part above the Bay
> And the heat of Summer dries the spots of rain
> Still falling:
> I am, here, now, where dark clouds of thunder
> Have given way to blue
> Such that the tide, turning,
> Begins to break my vow of distance
> Down.
>
> A women, there, whose dog, disobeying,
> Splashes sea with sand until new interest
> Takes him where
> This bearded man of greying hair
> No longer reeks

With sadness.
Instead:
The smile of joy when Sun of Summer
Presents again this Paradise of Earth
For I am only tears, falling

David Myatt
February 2012

Notes

[1] vv.879-886. The text is that of the Cotton Caligula MS in the British Library as transcribed by JWH Atkins in *The Owl and the Nightingale*, Cambridge University Press, 1922. The attempted rendering into modern English is by DWM.

Twenty Years Ago, Today

Twenty years ago today, someone whom I loved who loved me died, too young and having harmed no one. Died, leaving me bereft, if only for a while. For too soon my return to those hubriatic, selfish, suffering-causing, and extremist, ways of my pasts. As if, despite the grief, the pain of loss, I personally had learned nothing, except in such moments of such remembering that did not, unfortunately, impact too much upon my practicalities of life; at least until another bereavement, thirteen years later, came to shock, shake, betake me far from my arrogant presumptions about myself, about life, to thus lead, to so slowly lead, to this day now, when I on a clear cold day sit yet again interiorly dwelling on what, if anything, is our human purpose of being here and why such bereavements, such early deaths, just seem so unjust, unfair.

For they - as so many - having harmed no one, died, while I - as so many - lived on to continue causing mayhem, chaos, suffering, and grief, no God it seemed to stay us or to slay us for our miscreant mischief. That, to me, is no deity of empathy and compassion; only one explanation to maybe betake our grief, our tears, our fears, away.

For even now - having perhaps at least in some ways, and partially, understood the errors of both my selfish and my extremist pasts - I cannot seem to accept that such a compassionate, empathic, deity would, could, sanction, allow, such a taking of such innocence and such infliction of suffering to continue. It makes no sense to me, since I now cannot, it seems, believe there is another life awaiting us where we, judicium divinum, are rewarded or condemned. I find no comfort there; no satisfying explanation for the suffering that afflicts so many now as in the past: as if that, such suffering, as was written once, many times, is some sort of casus belli for our life, to be endured until such time as such a deity deems fit to end it.

> Man, that is born of a woman, hath but a short time to live, and is full of misery. He cometh up, and is cut down, like a flower; he fleeth as it were a shadow, and never continueth in one stay. In the midst of life we are in death. Of whom may we seek for succour, but of thee, O Lord...

Must we therefore be resigned to suffering, to misery, to injustices, to the iniquity, to the continuing iniquity, of selfish, hubriatic, individuals who bully, rape, scheme, subjugate, manipulate, injure, maim, and kill? Reassured by judicium divinum or - perhaps - hoping, trusting, in the pending justice of some judge, some government, or some State?

Am I still so arrogant, so unhumble, so unknowing, as to somehow desire such suffering to cease here, and now? Am I so wrong that I still feel the need for someone, some many, somewhere, to somehow in some way forestall, prevent, such deeds by such persons as may unjustly harm some others so that there is no waiting for the divine justice of a deity; no waiting for some Court somewhere to - possibly, and sometimes - requite a grievous wrong. No waiting for that promised idealistic idyllic future society when we humans, somehow - perhaps miraculously - changed in nature en masse, have ceased to so grievously, harmfully, selfishly, inflict ourselves on others.

My own and only fallible answer seems to be that of a personal honour. For each of us to gently try to carry that necessary harmony, that balance, of δίκη, wordlessly within; to thus restrain ourselves from causing harm while being able, prepared, in the immediacy of the moment, to personally, physically, restrain - prevent - others when we chance upon such harm being done. This, to me, is Life in its wholesome natural fullness - as lived, presenced, by the brief, mortal, consciously aware, emanations we are; mortal emanations capable of restraint, reason, culture, and reforming change; of learning from our pathei-mathos and that of others. My personal answer to personal questions, perplexion, and to grief and doubt. The answer which is to live in hope - even need - of a personal loyal love; to live with empathy, gentleness, humility, compassion, and yet with strength enough to do what should be done when, within the purvue of our personal space, we meet with one or many causing suffering and harm, no thought then for the fragility of our own mortal life or even for personal consequences beyond the ἁρμονίη we, in such honourable moments, are.

But is this possibly - probably - only a memory, only a fleeting memory, of the sadness-engendered hope felt in those long dark wakeful hours of last night?

David Myatt
2013

In Loving Remembrance of Sue, died 4th April 1993

Some Questions For DWM, 2017

Introductory Note: The following answers are replies to some of the questions submitted by two individuals through various third parties in 2017, which questions have been edited for publication, and are not in the order in which they were submitted.

∘∘∘

° In your article entitled *One viator among so many*, you say:

> "My hubriatic error in those extremist decades was essentially two-fold: (i) to aspire to bring-into-being some-thing that would not and could not, in centennial terms (let alone in millennial or cosmic terms) endure; and (ii) to use violence and incite hatred, intolerance, and killing, in order to try and presence that causal some-thing..."

Throughout your extremist decades, did you ever have certain moments of doubts where you inwardly felt that something was wrong about the abstractions you were cherishing at the time? Some sort of powerful, inward interventions that could be compared to the dream P. Cornelius Scipio has about Africanus in the beautiful writing of Cicero?

Until the late 1990's the only doubts I had were those connected with strategy and tactics and my own role in establishing a new society based on National-Socialist principles. Thus even when I ceased to be politically active - such as during my time in a monastery in the 1970's, during periods as a vagabond, and during the first few years of my first marriage - I remained a National-Socialist and never once doubted that National-Socialism was something other than good, noble, and necessary just as I never doubted that the story of the Shoah was other than a fabrication.

The doubts which did arise in the late 1990's were engendered by personal experiences, such as many trips to Egypt, working long hours outdoors on a farm, my arrest in early 1998 by Police officers from Scotland Yard followed by regular visits to Charing Cross Police station, interviews there, as part of my bail conditions; and several conversations with a Special Branch officer seconded to the city near where I was then living.

∘∘∘

° Considering the very active, diverse and even sometimes mystical life you've had, would it be right to assume that the Numinous Way/Philosophy of Pathei-Mathos is in some way the culmination of your being?

All that 'philosophy' seems to be to me now is a rather wordy and a rather egoistic, vainful, attempt to present what I (rightly or wrongly) believed I had learned about myself and the world as a result of various experiences. Which is why I in my solitude (and as a retiree) now concentrate on and have for a few years concentrated on translating tractates of the Corpus Hermeticum and the Gospel of John, living each day as it passes and unconcerned about what my being - and my relation to Being - is now or may be or perhaps should be. It was either translation, or returning to life as a vagabond which is something I might yet do.

∘ ∘ ∘

° In your article entitled *A Vagabond in Exile from the Gods*, you say:

> "For me, there is a knowing of how limited and fallible my knowledge and understanding are, combined with an intangible intimation of some-thing possibly existing which is so abstruse that any and all attempts - at least by me - to meld it into words, and thus form and confine it into some idea or ideas, would miss or distort its essence. An intimation of what terms such as 'acausal' and 'numinous' (and even θεός/θεοί) do little to describe, hinting as such terms do of externalities - of an 'out there' - whereas this some-thing is an intrinsic part of us, connecting us to all life, human, terran, and otherwise, and thus reveals our φύσις - our relation to beings and Being - behind the appearance that is our conception of our separate self. An intimation thus of our brief causality of mortal life being only one momentary microcosmic presencing of that-which we it seems have a faculty to apprehend, and a that-which which lives-on both before and after our brief moment of apprehended causal life."

You talk often about the fallibility of language in this text and many others such as *Perhaps words are the problem* and *The Love that needs no Words.* Such writings remind me of what Wittgenstein has once said: "Most human problems originate from us attempting to say the unsayable" [...]

Why do you believe human beings have this tendency to feel separate from everything instead of unified and why do you believe there is such an insisted importance for us as a species to manufacture abstractions? Also, you sometimes make use of the word 'categories' when it comes to language which tells me you studied Nelson Goodman and his theory of world making through language. Am I right in such assumption and if so, may I ask you what you thought of his research on language.

No, I have not studied the work of the person you mention with my use of the term 'categories' most probably deriving - if it derives from anything - from a study of various works by Plato and Aristotle and in particular the ἰδέα/εἶδος of Plato and Aristotle's criticisms of it.

In respect of human beings having "a tendency to feel separate from everything" all I saught to express was my own fallible intimation of - not a belief in - our apparent human tendency toward ipseity and toward the manufacture of abstractions in an attempt to understand ourselves, others, and the external world. Which intimation of mine is not original, not new, with the genesis of my intimation my forty or so years as a practical and violent extremist, as a propagandist, an ideologue, and a "theoretician of terror".

Does our human history and our personal experience reveal that the physis of we mortals is such that this tendency toward ipseity and the manufacture of abstractions is innate? My fallible intimation was that it does. Is the tendency that some mortals appear to have to balance ipseity and abstractions with wordless empathy also innate? Perhaps; but I really do not know although my intimation was that the tendency toward the balance that wordless empathy could engender was and is often found more in women than in men. What does - or would or perhaps should - this mean in terms of society and the cessation of suffering? Again, I do not know and have no answers, only more fallible intimations one of which is that even 'empathy' as I construe it, as well as descriptors [1] of mine such as masculous and muliebral, may of themselves be manufactured abstractions. If so, my weltanschauung (which I initially and somewhat hubriatically termed the 'philosophy' of pathei-mathos) is fundamentally flawed. So it is perhaps just as well that I now concern myself with translations.

○○○

° In your article entitled *A Learning From Physis* you say:

> "Thus it is that I find, through and because of such a recalling, that what I value now, what I feel and sense is most important, is a direct, personal, mutual love between two human beings – and that such love is far far more important, more real, more human, than any abstraction, than any idealism, than any so-called duty, than any dogma, than any cause, however "idealistic"; more important – far more important – than any ideology, than any and all -isms and -ologies be such -isms and such -ologies understood conventionally as political, or religious or social. For it is the desire to love, to be loved – and the desire to cease to cause suffering – which are important, which should be our priority, and which are the true measure of our own humanity."

[...]

In accordance with your own words, would you say that love has indeed all the metaphysical properties to vanquish abstractions or dilute them and that love provides an authentic 'empathical' mode of wordless communication between two beings?

An interesting question and my fallible intimation - derived from my own experience - is that the intuitive wordless knowing that is empathy is somewhat different from the personal emotion or the deep personal affection that the term 'love' often describes, although empathy can be (again in my experience) the genesis of, and supportive of, such personal love. But the emotion engendered by personal love can also cause suffering both of the person who loves and in regard to the one loved, especially if there is not a mutual, loyal, equality of love.

Empathy - assuming it is a descriptor and not an abstraction - is or seems to me to be somewhat temperate and thus not involving the intense and very personal emotion toward another person that personal love often involves. Rather, it could be considered a different type of 'love' analogous - not identical - to how many people over millennia have described compassion as a kind of 'love' (or as loving-kindness) and how some others, and mystics especially, have described their love for certain religious figures such as Jesus of Nazareth, the Blessed Virgin Mary, and the Prophet Muhammad. For there seems to me in such a 'mystical' love a move away from ipseity, revealed as that moving away is - again, in my experience - by a certain personal humility.

ooo

° I always felt that the Numinous Way (the philosophy of Pathei-Mathos) was heavily inspired by what is most pure in ancient religious/esoteric texts. Good examples of this are: The Corpus Hermeticum, Somnium Scipionis, The Gospel of John, Oedipus Tyrannus, and Aeschylus - to name only a few. I recall reading in *Myngath* that you became accustomed to certain of these ancestral authors in your youth, and so I was wondering what made you drift toward abstractions anyway and ignore the 'lessons' - as stated in your article entitled "A slowful learning, perhaps"- about hubris which are contained in those ancient texts?

I can remember as a schoolboy in the Far East reading Thucydides (in Greek, with Liddell and Scott's Intermediate Lexicon to hand if required) while sitting in the shade near a beach on which the South China Sea ebbed and flowed. Many days later on the same beach - and interspersed with drinking bottles of a certain carbonated sugar-filled drink and swimming out to and back from where (if my ageing memory is correct) a 'shark net' was strategically placed - the book read was the Iliad, followed days later by the Odyssey, then by Herodotus.

While I did peruse the works of Plato and Aristotle, what I imbibed in those early years from such books of Ancient Hellas was nothing particularly philosophical but instead martial, and I could not but help admire those 'thinking warriors', those 'perspicacious inventive gentlemen' (περιφραδὴς ἀνήρ as Sophocles described them, cunning in inventive arts who arrive now with dishonour and then with honour, τι τὸ μηχανόεν τέχνας ὑπὲρ ἐλπίδ᾽ἔχων τοτὲ μὲν κακόν, ἄλλοτ᾽ ἐπ᾽ ἐσθλὸν ἕρπει) nurtured as I was then and had been for years by and in various colonies and outposts of what was still the British Empire. Thus it was natural that when, a short time later, I first learned about the Third Reich and about the loyalty of a soldier such as Otto Ernst Remer and the heroic actions of warriors such as Leon Degrelle I admired such men and intuited that something of the warrior ethos of ancient Hellas and Sparta may have manifested itself in our modern world.

In brief, I - in my arrant presumptive youthfulness - glossed over the deeper philosophical meanings, especially concerning hubris.

ooo

° In Myngath, your poems and your letters, you share with us the terrible ordeal which you had to go through twice in your life; the loss of your companion. Would you say that Pathei-Mathos is sometimes the only antidote that can shatter abstractions and awaken once more what is truly important in life?

All I know is that it was a personal trauma that forced me to confront myself for who and what I was. In the hours following the tragic death of a loved one in 2006 I was so starkly reminded of the tragic death of another loved one some thirteen years before and how I felt in the hours, the days, after her death in 1993. I on that day in May in 2006 knew - starkly, gravely, bitterly, beyond words - that I had learned nothing meaningful in the intervening thirteen years. It was as if in those intervening years - when I pontificated, when I sallied hatefully violently forth on behalf of one abstraction after another and incited hatred, violence, and terrorism, and caused others to suffer and die - I had sullied, demeaned, the life, the suffering, the love, the death, of a woman (Sue) who had never harmed anyone in her whole life and who had loved me in a simple, genuine, unaffected, loyal way. I just intuitively understood that they - those two woman who died too young - were far better human beings than I was or could ever hope to be.

According to my limited knowledge and experience, pathei-mathos has over millennia and recently changed some others in a positive way (where by positive I mean toward being honourable and empathic), but as to whether it can change sufficient people to bring an end to or significantly reduce the suffering we humans continue to inflict upon each other, via abstractions, egoism, and otherwise, I do not know.

o o o

° You talk often of space colonization and science-fiction and how such an idea was what fuelled certain of your abstractions when you were an impetuous young man. Reflecting on your youth and considering what you wrote in your article entitled *Education and Pathei-Mathos*, do you believe that it would be more sensible for us as a species to settle our disputes here and now and then seek to expand our presence on other planets?

I do rather vaguely recall pontificating a few years ago about whether we as a species should, given what I surmised was our suffering-causing physis, inflict ourselves on territories beyond Earth, and whether such an adventure might be the maturing experience we as a species require.

But it is all, at least on my part, speculation, founded on certain assumptions and intimations, which assumptions and intimations, given that they are mine, might well be - and probably are - wrong.

o o o

° If you could go back through time and talk to the younger version of yourself, what would you say to this daring and impetuous young man?

As a young man and as a young boy I was arrogant and rebellious, and adverse to taking advice. So perhaps whatever I would say to that young man - or that boy - he would either not understand or not appreciate. As I wrote to a correspondent in 2012 regarding encountering some young men who had political affiliations and views similar to the ones I had and held decades ago:

> "Would I, some forty years ago, have listened to some old man pontificating about his experiences, his life, his learning? I doubt it. For I then, as they now, had that certainty-of-knowing, that arrogance, that is one of the foundations of extremism, of whatever kind." [2]

○○○

° I know that you studied many different religious avenues throughout your life and immersed yourself in different cultures. Would you say that religion as a whole is an attempt at cosmic unity but is unfortunately tainted by the same problems when it comes to language and denotatum which creates a continual separation between a group and another which then cause conflicts and sufferings?

I feel that all I can - and should - do is to try to answer such a question based on my own personal experience. Which is that all mainstream religions seem to me to try and express a similar central insight regarding our mortal nature and our relation to the Cosmos and to Being, however Being is described, denoted. However, they also seem to manifest or to develope over centuries, and in varying degrees, the duality inherent in our physis - the duality of sometimes alleviating suffering and sometimes of causing suffering, directly or indirectly - and that partly because of how a particular religion is or comes to be interpreted (or misinterpreted) by we fallible mortals. Sometimes, for instance, people with good intentions, through their intervention or interference, cause or contribute to suffering.

In addition, their central insight is overwhelmingly embodied in words, in denotatum, often written down in some book or in some compilations as is the case for example with Christianity, Islam, Hinduism, and Buddhism. And words are subject to interpretation and misinterpretation, especially when translated from one language to another. Even when there is an extant aural tradition, as in Taoism and certain Buddhist traditions, by its nature the tradition has to be expressed through the medium of words which may or may not, depending on the teacher or master, convey something of its essence and which may or may not be a distortion, over centuries, of the original essence.

Of those religions which have methods which transcend words - such as the Christian contemplative (mystic) tradition, the Satori of Zen Buddhism, and the Dhikr of the Sufi - they by their nature represent only a minority of believers, with what is wordless revealed, to the individual, through those methods is often, in my experience, wordfully conveyed - or is attempted to be conveyed - by the individual to experienced others so that the insight, the revealing, can be confirmed.

All of which led me to conclude that while mainstream religions seem on balance over centuries to have been and continue to be forces for good - striving as they do to place mortals into a Cosmic perspective - I personally no longer find them a satisfactory answer to the question of suffering or providefull of a satisfactory understanding of our mortal physis and thus of what may be required for us to consciously change ourselves for the better.

ooo

° In your articles, you often quote T.S Eliot beautiful segment:

> We shall not cease from exploration
> And the end of all our exploring
> Will be to arrive where we started
> And know the place for the first time.

Would you say this segment is extremely representative of what the Greek word Ἀνοδος means and would you say it is also very appropriate to describe the synthesis of your life when reflecting on your extremist past?

Those poetic words of TS Eliot certainly do, for me, express something of what I have discovered about myself after some forty years of diverse peregrinations. Which peregrinations do seem in retrospect to have similarities to what the term ἄνοδος describes and denotes in certain Hellenistic metaphysical traditions and in the Poemandres tractate of the Corpus Hermeticum even though my peregrinations were unplanned, the mostly wilful but sometimes unwilful journeyings and explorations of an arrant, selfish and arrogant, individual who certainly does not believe or assume that he, after decades, has achieved some sort of a 'synthesis'.

Instead, my supposition is of still being flawed, of still learning; of still striving - and so often failing - each day to live as I feel I should, as an honourable, compassionate, tolerant, person wordlessly aware of and appreciative of the numinous.

ooo

° [...] Like most people, I went through certain saddening experiences in my life and was deeply hurt at some point or another. What would you say can cure this feeling of separation, of fear and of defensiveness that most people seem to harbor after going through Pathei-Mathos -

ultimately losing touch with who they authentically are? If your answer is correlative with the values found in the Numinous Way as you seem to suggest (love, compassion, tolerance, non-interference, humility), how then do you bear your reclusive expiation?

Naturally, I would suggest the tentative answers expressed by my weltanschauung: the answers of compassion, empathy, tolerance, humility, a personal and loyal and shared love, and of personal honour.

My somewhat eremitic way of life is a natural, a necessary, consequence of my past. Of knowing my past mistakes, the suffering caused, and how selfish and hubriatic I was for so many decades. As I wrote, in 2012, to the aforementioned correspondent,

> "I simply do not trust myself anymore not to cause suffering, not to make even more mistakes, not to show poor judgement again [...] I am not - by being reclusive - retreating from the world, just seeking not to inflict my error-prone self on the world, on others. An error-prone self, a person, I admit I now do not like very much. Which is why there is also no longer any desire, not even any secret desire, to share my life, in however small or complete a way, with anyone or even with others be they friends old or new."

∘∘∘

° In several of your articles including in Myngath, you talk about the importance of φύσις and the species of time. Also, you talk about how you have an appreciation for rural communities and how these communities sometimes have a wordless appreciation of the cosmos and share an aural tradition which originated decades if not centuries ago [...]

Would you say that such a perspective is slowly being lost because of our modern way of living and that this lack of contact with the wordless, with nature, will cause more abstractions and thus, more suffering? If so, do you believe that such a rural way of living facilitates a journeying (both as an individual person and as a collectivity) toward Wu-Wei and a restoration of δίκη?

My fallible intimation - which yet again is nothing original or new - is that such a wordless perception of the Cosmos, and especially of Nature, is indeed being slowly lost for a variety of reasons. One reason seems to be an increasing dependence on technology and machines over and above crafts and work which require both a certain skill and the use of one's hands and hand-held tools, which crafts and work involve a certain careful, and slow, and often a toiling way of working. Another reason is a lack of direct, personal, and rural contact with Nature over the Seasons of many years, which rural closeness - through a working-there or a dwelling-there for years - reveals the natural rhythms of Nature and the Cosmos beyond, one of which rhythms is the process of balance, manifest as this sometimes is in good seasons, in bad seasons, and in birth, living, work, and death. Another reason is that for so many in the modern West there is no longer an ancestral culture of which one is a living, dwelling, part - a connexion between the past and the future and a connexion with a rural place of dwelling - and which culture preserves the slowly learned wisdom of the past, manifest as that often is in aurally and personally learning what is right, what is wrong, and thus how one should behave in order to maintain the natural balance of life. Instead there are external influences, changeable, and changing, manufactured and disposable, often material and egoistical and hubriatic in ethos and increasingly being rapidly relayed through various types of readily accessible media.

Apart from a few years lived in two cities and a few years lived in towns, I have spent my childhood and adult life in rural areas, from Africa to the Far East, to the rural Shires of England. Some of my happiest memories are working with my hands, outdoors, on farms and as a gardener. So perhaps I have acquired a certain bias, perhaps even a prejudice against modern urbanized living.

○○○

° Heraclitus once said that: "Man is most nearly himself when he achieves the seriousness of a child at play." I enjoyed your translation of Heraclitus as I did enjoy all your other translations and I wanted to know what do you think of this quote at the point you are at in your life presently?

Since I cannot find anything resembling that quotation in the Greek texts that I have of the extant fragments attributed to Heraclitus, I am unable to comment on it in relation to Heraclitus.

The nearest I can find is fragment 52, with the text from *Fragmente der Vorsokratiker*, edited H. Diels, published in Berlin in 1903:

αἰὼν παῖς ἐστι παίζων πεσσεύων· παιδὸς ἡ βασιληίη

With my translation (or rather interpretation of meaning) being,

"For Aion, we are a game, pieces moved on some board: since, in this world of ours, we are but children."

Where I take the sense of βασίλειος metaphorically and poetically - not literally - and thus as referring to the 'dominion', the 'kingdom' we believe we mortals (in our hubris) 'royally inhabit' rather than literally meaning some sort of "royal or kingly power". A conventional translation - which in my opinion and like many translations of the fragments ignores the poetry and the humour found in the sayings attributed to Heraclitus - is, "Eternity is a child playing draughts, the kingly power is a child's."

In respect of this fragment, some of my insights are a poor echo of that particular ancient apprehension.

∘∘∘

° In your essay *On Minutiae And The Art Of Revision* you wrote that "as someone with a rather paganus weltanschauung, brought-into-being by πάθει μάθος, but respectful still of other manifestations of the numinous, I strive to understand that Gospel [of John] in the cultural milieu of the ancient Roman Empire."

Would I be right in thinking that your philosophy of pathei-mathos is pagan in the Western tradition since you have written that your weltanschauung is the philosophy of pathei-mathos?

In many ways that philosophy does reflect the paganus tradition of the Greco-Roman world as described, for example, by the following paraphrase of Cicero which I included in the Introduction of my translation of tractate XII of the Corpus Hermeticum. Ancient European paganism, in its essence, involved:

> an apprehension of the complete unity (a cosmic order, κόσμος, mundus) beyond the apparent parts of that unity, together with the perceiveration that we mortals – albeit a mere and fallible part of the unity – have been gifted with our existence so that we may perceive and understand this unity, and, having so perceived, may ourselves seek to be whole, and thus become as balanced (perfectus), as harmonious, as the unity itself. [3]

However, the paganus tradition of my weltanschauung is also mystical and contemplative in the sense that there is a wordless appreciation of the numinous and an apprehension, through the wordless knowing of empathy, of Being and beings with this apprehension being personal, for by means of empathy my assumption is that we can:

> "understand both φύσις and Πόλεμος, and thus apprehend Being as Being, and the nature of beings - and in particular the nature of our being, as mortals. For empathy reveals to us the acausality of Being and thus how the process of abstraction, involving as it does an imposition of causality and separation upon beings (and the ideation implicit in opposites and dialectic), is a covering-up of Being." [4]

Furthermore, "the apparent parts of the unity" are expressed by descriptors such as masculous and muliebral, with that unity - The One, μονάς - not designated by terms such as theos (God, god) or theoi (gods) but rather metaphysically, as Being and the emanations/effluvia of Being such as ourselves, Nature, and the Cosmos itself.

° Would I be right in thinking that your philosophy - or weltanschauung as you prefer to call it - is indebted to hermeticism as described in the ancient Hermetica and if so is that why you have translated many of those texts?

Yes, some aspects of some of the tractates of the Corpus Hermeticum have influenced my thinking, just as Aristotle, Aeschylus, Sophocles, Marcus Aurelius, and other classical and Hellenistic Greek and Latin writers have. I first read the Corpus Hermeticum - in the Latin of Marsilii Ficini - when a monk, with the Greek text - by Parthey [5] - being read some months later. When I came to re-read the tractates, sometime around 2011, I decided to begin translating those that interested me since I found existing translations unhelpful and somewhat misleading given their propensity to employ words such as God/god and 'good' and 'evil' and given the underlying assumption that many or most of those tractates were influenced by early Christianity rather than, as I had presumed when I first read them, of early Christianity probably being influenced by the diverse hermetic traditions which existed and flourished during the Hellenistic period.

∘∘∘

° Since 2012 when you revised your 'numinous way' into the philosophy of pathei-mathos you have written several essays on diverse philosophical topics which expand on what you have published in books like *The Numinous Way of Pathei-Mathos*. I'm thinking here of new essays like *Perhaps Words Are The Problem* and *A Note On Greek Terms In The Philosophy Of Pathei-Mathos*. Do you intend to write more essays and to explain your philosophy in greater detail and if so are the new essays going to be published in a new collection?

In the past I have indeed written a lot about many things. But there has been too much writing, too much pontificating, about too many things, and my post-2011 writings are no exception. My only - quite feeble - excuse for the plenitude of such post-2011 writings is that they, through the act of writing and corresponding with others, were partly expiative but mostly aided (or seemed to me to aid) my understanding of myself particularly in relation to my extremist past and the religions I had personal and practical experience of. But in retrospect those post-2011 writings - including *Myngath* and works such as the book *The Numinous Way of Pathei-Mathos* - now just seem so vain.

Thus, as to whether I will write more metaphysical or even more personal essays, I have to be honest and reply with "no" even though I am aware that the 'philosophy' of pathei-mathos, as described in works such as *The Numinous Way of Pathei-Mathos* and scattered in numerous other essays is not expounded as clearly and precisely as it could and perhaps should be. And a "no" to further writings because I have become ever more aware of the consequences of words, of my own fallibility; of the depth of my uncertainty of knowing; of how words - including mine - can and often do obscure the wordless empathic essence; and especially aware of how such essays can be, and in my case seem to have been, manifestations of vanity and occasionally of hubris. Thus, these answers of mine to submitted questions will be the last.

In this respect, receiving and attempting to answer such questions as have been submitted this past year has been most helpful to me, another learning experience, providing a renewed acceptance of such greater solitude as will hopefully prevent me from any further pontifications public and private, with my translations, slowly proceeding as they are, becoming my only occasional vainful presence in the outer world, for such translations are somewhat other-worldly, and neutral at least in respect of opinions about matters which I now accept are beyond my purview, with my much self-vaunted 'diverse experience over decades' no longer seeming to me to be a viable excuse for inflicting my presumptions and intimations on others.

∘ ∘ ∘

[1] A descriptor is defined, in *The Numinous Way of Pathei-Mathos*, as

> a word, a term, used to describe some-thing which exists and which is personally observed, or is discovered, by means of our senses (including the faculty of empathy). A descriptor differs from an ideation, category, or abstraction, in that a descriptor describes what-is as 'it' is observed, according to its physis (its nature) whereas an abstraction, for example, denotes what is presumed/assumed/idealized, past or present or future. A descriptor relies on, is derived from, describes, individual knowing and individual judgement; an abstraction relies on something abstract, impersonal, such as some opinion/knowing/judgement of others or some assumptions, theory, or hypothesis made by others.

[2] Extracts from the 2012 letters were published, in 2013, in the book *Understanding and Rejecting Extremism: A Very Strange Peregrination*.

[3] A paraphrase of what Cicero wrote on the subject, which was:

> "Neque enim est quicquam aliud praeter mundum quoi nihil absit quodque undique aptum atque perfectum expletumque sit omnibus suis numeris et partibus [...] ipse autem homo ortus est ad mundum contemplandum et imitandum – nullo modo perfectus, sed est quaedam particula perfecti." M. Tullius Cicero, *De Natura Deorum*, Liber Secundus, xiii, xiv, 37

[4] *The Abstraction of Change as Opposites and Dialectic*. Included in *The Numinous Way of Pathei-Mathos*. 2013.

[5] G. Parthey. *Poemander*. Berlin. 1854.

Cantio Arcana

Introductory Note

A (non-literal) translation of the ancient Esoteric Song from sections 17 and 18 of tractate XIII of the Corpus Hermeticum, entitled as that tractate is:

Ερμού του τρισμεγίστου προς τον υιόν Τάτ
εν όρει λόγος απόκρυφος περί παλιγγενεσίας και σιγής επαγγελίας

On A Mountain:
Hermes Trismegistus To His Son Thoth,
An Esoteric Discourse Concerning Palingenesis
And The Requirement of Silence

Given the content, the song is pagan and without any Christian influence, although it has been described by some scholars as 'gnostic' in nature. For reasons of readability - and because of the songful nature of the text - I have divided the translation into (somewhat arbitrary) verses.

The Greek text used is that of A.D. Nock & A-J. Festugiere, *Corpus Hermeticum*, Tome II, Third Edition, 1972, and the references to other tractates are to my respective translations and commentaries.

ooo

Text

πᾶσα φύσις κόσμου προσδεχέσθω τοῦ ὕμνου τὴν ἀκοήν. ἀνοίγηθι γῆ, ἀνοιγήτω μοι πᾶς μοχλὸς ἀβύσσου, τὰ δένδρα μὴ σείεσθε. ὑμνεῖν μέλλω τὸν τῆς κτίσεως κύριον, καὶ τὸ πᾶν καὶ τὸ ἕν. ἀνοίγητε οὐρανοί, ἄνεμοί τε στῆτε. ὁ κύκλος ὁ ἀθάνατος τοῦ θεοῦ, προσδεξάσθω μου τὸν λόγον· μέλλω γὰρ ὑμνεῖν τὸν κτίσαντα τὰ πάντα, τὸν πήξαντα τὴν γῆν καὶ οὐρανὸν κρεμάσαντα καὶ ἐπιτάξαντα ἐκ τοῦ ὠκεανοῦ τὸ γλυκὺ ὕδωρ εἰς τὴν οἰκουμένην καὶ ἀοίκητον ὑπάρχειν εἰς διατροφὴν καὶ κτίσιν πάντων τῶν ἀνθρώπων, τὸν ἐπιτάξαντα πῦρ φανῆναι εἰς πᾶσαν πρᾶξιν θεοῖς τε καὶ ἀνθρώποις. δῶμεν πάντες ὁμοῦ αὐτῷ τὴν εὐλογίαν, τῷ ἐπὶ τῶν οὐρανῶν μετεώρῳ, τῷ πάσης φύσεως κτίστῃ.

οὗτός ἐστιν ὁ τοῦ νοῦ ὀφθαλμός, καὶ δέξαιτο τῶν δυνάμεών μου τὴν εὐλογίαν. αἱ δυνάμεις αἱ ἐν ἐμοί, ὑμνεῖτε τὸ ἓν καὶ τὸ πᾶν· συνάσατε τῷ θελήματί μου πᾶσαι αἱ ἐν ἐμοὶ δυνάμεις. γνῶσις ἁγία, φωτισθεὶς ἀπὸ σοῦ, διὰ σοῦ τὸ νοητὸν φῶς ὑμνῶν χαίρω ἐν χαρᾷ νοῦ. πᾶσαι δυνάμεις ὑμνεῖτε σὺν ἐμοί. καὶ σύ μοι, ἐγκράτεια, ὕμνει. δικαιοσύνη μου, τὸ δίκαιον ὕμνει δι᾽ ἐμοῦ. κοινωνία ἡ ἐμή, τὸ πᾶν ὕμνει δι᾽ ἐμοῦ· ὕμνει ἀλήθεια τὴν ἀλήθειαν. τὸ ἀγαθόν, ἀγαθόν, ὕμνει· ζωὴ καὶ φῶς, ἀφ᾽ ὑμῶν εἰς ὑμᾶς χωρεῖ ἡ εὐλογία. εὐχαριστῶ σοι, πάτερ, ἐνέργεια τῶν δυνάμεων. εὐχαριστῶ σοι, θεέ, δύναμις τῶν ἐνεργειῶν μου· ὁ σὸς Λόγος δι᾽ ἐμοῦ ὑμνεῖ σέ. δι᾽ ἐμοῦ δέξαι τὸ πᾶν λόγῳ, λογικὴν θυσίαν.

Translation

Let every Physis of Kosmos favourably listen to this song.
Gaia: be open, so that every defence against the Abyss is opened for me;
Trees: do not incurvate;
For I now will sing for the Master Artisan,
For All That Exists, and for The One.

Open: you Celestial Ones; and you, The Winds, be calm.
Let the deathless clan of theos accept this, my logos.
For I shall sing of the maker of everything;
Of who established the Earth,
Of who affixed the Heavens,
Of who decreed that Oceanus should bring forth sweet water
To where was inhabited and where was uninhabited
To so sustain all mortals;
Of who decreed that Fire should bring light
To divinities and mortals for their every use.

Let us all join in fond celebration of who is far beyond the Heavens:
That artisan of every Physis.

May the one who is the eye of perceiveration accept this fond celebration
From my Arts.
Let those Arts within me sing for The One and for All That Exists
As I desire all those Arts within me to blend, together.

Numinous knowledge, from you a numinal understanding:
Through you, a song of apprehended phaos,
Delighted with delightful perceiverance.
Join me, all you Arts, in song.

You, mastery, sing; and you, respectful of custom,
Through me sing of such respect.
Sing, my companions, for All That Exists:
Honesty, through me, sing of being honest,
The noble, sing of nobility.

Phaos and Life: fond celebration spreads from us to you.

My gratitude, father: actuosity of those my Arts.
My gratitude, theos: Artisan of my actuosities;
Through me, the Logos is sung for you.

Through me, may All That Exists accept
Such respectful wordful offerings as this.

Commentary

every Physis of Kosmos. Among the presencings of the Kosmos described here by their physis are Earth, Trees, the Heavens, Air, and Water.

In respect of Kosmos and physis, qv. tractate XII:14,

> ἀνάγκη δὲ καὶ ἡ πρόνοια καὶ ἡ φύσις ὄργανά ἐστι τοῦ κόσμου
>
> Necessitas, forseeing, and physis, are implements of Kosmos

song. ὕμνος. Not a 'hymn' in the Christian sense (which the word hymn now so often imputes) but rather celebrating the numinous, and theos, in song, verse (ode), and chant.

Gaia. γῆ. Earth as elemental principle, hence the personification here since Earth is being directly, personally, invoked.

open. ἀνοίγνυμι. Cf. Papyri Graecae Magicae, XXXVI. 312ff. The term was often used in both mystic odes and in classical magicae incantations. The Latin *aperio* well expresses the sense, as in "aperire librum et septem signacula eius," (Jerome, Revelation V:5) and "et cum aperuisset sigillum secundum." (Jerome, Revelation VI:3)

μοχλός. Here, not a literal 'bolt' or 'lock' but what prevents (access to) or is a defence against something.

Abyss. ἀβύσσου. This is the emendation of Reitzenstein for the various readings of the MSS. Nock has ὄμβρου which does not make sense here, for why "open what prevents" rain? In respect of ἄβυσσος, qv. tractate III:1.

incurvate. This unusual English term is appropriate here to poetically suggest the sense of the Greek - σείω - which is to bend from side to side as if shaken by an earthquake, by a trembling of the Earth.

Master Artisan. κτίσεως κύριον. 'Founding Lord', or less poetically, Lord of Creation. Theos as creator-artisan is mentioned in Poemandres 9, with the term there, and in tractate IV:1, being δημιουργόν. Qv. also δύναμις δὲ τοῦ θεοῦ ὁ αἰών (the craft of theos: Aion) in tractate XI:3.

All That Exists. τὸ πᾶν. Qv. tractate XII: 22.

clan. κύκλος. Here signifying a particular group, or a particular assembly, of people as in the English expression "the inner circle." Hence, "the clan of theos".

Sweet water. γλυκὺ ὕδωρ. The sweetness of water suitable to drink.

bring light to. In respect of φαίνω as 'bringing light', cf. Plato, Timaeus, 39b,

> φῶς ὁ θεὸς ἀνῆψεν ἐν τῇ πρὸς γῆν δευτέρᾳ τῶν περιόδων, ὃ δὴ νῦν κεκλήκαμεν ἥλιον, ἵνα ὅτι μάλιστα εἰς ἅπαντα φαίνοι τὸν οὐρανὸν

> theos ignited a light in that second circle from Earth, named now as Helios, so that it could bring light to all of the heavens

fond celebration. Regarding εὐλογία in a neutral way which does not impute the Christian sense of "praise the Lord", qv. Poemandres 22,

> παραγίνομαι αὐτὸς ἐγὼ ὁ Νοῦς τοῖς ὁσίοις καὶ ἀγαθοῖς καὶ καθαροῖς καὶ ἐλεήμοσι, τοῖς εὐσεβοῦσι, καὶ ἡ παρουσία μου γίνεται βοήθεια, καὶ εὐθὺς τὰ πάντα γνωρίζουσι καὶ τὸν πατέρα ἱλάσκονται ἀγαπητικῶς καὶ εὐχαριστοῦσιν εὐλογοῦντες καὶ ὑμνοῦντες τεταγμένως πρὸς αὐτὸν τῇ στοργῇ

> I, perceiveration, attend to those of respectful deeds, the honourable, the refined, the compassionate, those aware of the numinous; to whom my being is a help so that they soon acquire knowledge of the whole and are affectionately gracious toward the father, fondly celebrating in song his position.

perceiveration. νοῦς. As in the Poemandres tractate and other tractates.

my Arts. As at Poemandres 31 - which is also a traditional doxology (δοξολογία) to theos - the sense of δυνάμεων is not 'powers', forces (or something similar and equally at variance with such a laudation) but 'arts'; that is, particular abilities, qualities, and skills. Here, these abilities and skills - the craft - relate to esoteric song; to be able to be an effective laudator in respect of theos and "every Physis of Kosmos."

numinous. ἅγιος. As in the Poemandres tractate and other tractates.

knowledge. As at Poemandres 26, γνῶσις here could be transliterated as gnosis although I incline toward the view that such a transliteration might - given what the term gnosis now imputes, as for example in being a distinct 'spiritual way' - lead to incorrectly imposing modern meanings on the text.

numinal understanding. φωτίζω here implies an understanding given by a divinity, as for example in spiritual enlightenment, something that is not conveyed if a single word such as 'enlightened' is used as a translation. In order to express something of the Greek, I had used the term 'numinal understanding' with numinal implying 'divine' as at tractate III:1,

> Δόξα πάντων ὁ θεὸς καὶ θεῖον καὶ φύσις θεία
> The numen of all beings is theos: numinal, and of numinal physis.

phaos. As at Poemandres 4ff - and in other tractates - a transliteration of φῶς - using the the Homeric φάος, given that it (like physis) is a fundamental principle of Hermetic weltanschauungen and one which the overused English word 'light', with all its modern and Christian interpretations, does not satisfactorily express.

mastery. Implying mastery over one's self, cf. Chaucer, The Physician's Tale: "Bacus hadde of hir mouth right no maistrie." (v. 58)

respectful of custom. δίκαιος. Not 'righteous', which imposes abstract theological meanings (derived from the Old Testament) on the text, but rather 'respectful of custom', of dutifully doing one's duty (that is, being honourable) toward both the gods and other mortals.

Honesty. ἀλήθεια. Given that those who are urged to sing are personifications, this is not some abstract, disputable, 'truth' but as often elsewhere in classical literature, a revealing, a dis-covering, of what is real as opposed to what is apparent or outer appearance. In personal terms, being honest and truthful.

actuosity. ἐνέργεια. Qv. tractate XII:21. The English term actuosity derives from the classical Latin actuosus and expresses the Greek here better than the word 'energy' given the modern connotations of that word. The meaning is of (often vigorous) activity or occurrences either natural or which result from the actions of divinities or daimons. Here, there are the actuosities of theos and of the mortal who uses their arts, their skill, in laudation.

respectful wordful offerings. Qv. Poemandres 31. The difficult to translate Greek term λογικὴν θυσίαν implies an offering, and one which is both respectful and conveyed by means of words but which words are of themselves insufficient, inadequate, with the term 'wordful' suggesting such insufficiency.

Appendix I

A Note On Greek Terms In The Philosophy Of Pathei-Mathos

As I mentioned in the *A Philosophical Compendiary* chapter of my book *The Numinous Way of Pathei-Mathos*, my philosophy of pathei-mathos has connexions to the culture of ancient Greece, exemplified by the many Greek terms and phrases I use in an attempt to express certain philosophical concepts. Such use of such terms also serves to intimate that my philosophy has some connexion to the Graeco-Roman mystical, and paganus, traditions, one of which traditions is outlined in the Ιερός Λόγος tractate of the Corpus Hermeticum where it is written that

> "...every psyche - embodied in flesh - can
> By the mirificence of the circumferent deities coursing the heavens
> Apprehend the heavens, and honour, and physis presenced, and the works of theos;
> Can understand divine influence as wyrdful change
> And thus, regarding what is good and what is bad, discover all the arts of honour."
> [1]

Furthermore, I also - and perhaps (as you mention) somewhat confusingly - use certain Greek and Latin terms in a specific way, such that the meaning I assign to them is not necessarily identical to how they were understood in classical times or the same as the meaning ascribed to them in modern Greek and Latin lexicons. A few examples being συμπάθεια, δίκη, φύσις, ἁρμονίη, perfectus, ἅγιος, and σωφρονεῖν.

Thus I understand ἅγιος - qv. my translation of and commentary on the Pœmandres tractate of the Corpus Hermeticum - not as the conventional 'holy'/sacred but rather as implying the numinous/numinosity, for I incline toward the view that the English words holy and sacred have too many modern connotations, Christian and otherwise, whereas numinous/numinosity still have the advantage of being religiously neutral and thus can intimate what an ancient paganus tradition may well have intimated. Hence also why and for example I in that tractate chose to translate ἀρχέτυπον εἶδος as 'quidditas of semblance' [2] rather than use (as some other translators have) an expression that included the word 'archetype' since that word has modern connotations that detract from (that can falsify) the meaning of the original Greek.

Another example, from the many, is φύσις which I use contextually to refer to not only its Homeric and later Aristotelian sense - of personal character, Nature, and the unfolding/change of being, respectively [3] - but also to what I have philosophically described as the unity (the being/Being) beyond the division of our φύσις, as individual mortals, into masculous and muliebral and a division we have made via abstractions (including 'forms'; the ἰδέα/εἶδος of Plato) and denotatum.

Yet another example is σωφρονεῖν which I use - in preference to σωφρονέω/σωφροσύνη - as a synonym for "a fair and balanced personal, individual, judgement" (that is, thoughtful reasoning, or wisdom) whereas in classical and Hellenic terms the expression should be τὸ σωφρονεῖν/εἰς τὸ σωφρονεῖν which imply 'to be discreet (Ag. 1425), being moderate, having good judgement', and so on. Here, as with Δίκα (in preference to δίκη) I have used a form or variant of a specific Greek word in order to suggest a modern philosophical meaning (or principle) and differentiate it from the conventional lexicographic meaning. But it would perhaps, with the hindsight of some years, have been better to avoid confusion and instead given and then used transliterations - sophronein, Dika - as I did (following the example of Jung) with ἐναντιοδρομίας/enantiodromia. That is, using the transliterations as Anglicized terms, as I do with my usage of πάθει μάθος - especially when the transliteration is employed - for such Anglicized terms do not follow the correct Greek grammatical (inflective) usage, with my writings thus employing expressions such as "a pathei-mathos", "that pathei-mathos", "which pathei-mathos", "our accumulated pathei-mathos", "my pathei-mathos", and of course "the philosophy of pathei-mathos".

In other words, my usage of some Greek terms - and the meaning I assign to some others - is somewhat idiosyncratic, often philosophical; and although I have endeavoured to explain my usage and meaning in essays and commentaries, obviously this has not always been successful or as pedantic as it perhaps should have been.

Thus when I, some years ago now, first published my translation of fragment 1 of Heraclitus - without commentary - it led to a Greek scholar, then in Oxford, to ask about my seeming neglect of ἀεὶ. In correspondence I explained my usage, later incorporating part of that correspondence into a brief commentary which I appended to the translation, writing in the commentary that "in my view, *tend to* captures the poetic sense of ἀεὶ here. That is, the literal - the bland, strident - 'always' is discarded in favour of a more Heraclitean expression of human beings having an apparently rather irreconcilable tendency - both now and as in the past - to ignore (or forget or not understand) certain things, even after matters have been explained to them (they have heard the explanation) and even after they have discovered certain truths for themselves." [4]

Therefore, and as I mentioned in the introduction to my *Poemandres*, some may well consider the words of Diogenes Laertius about Plato - *Lives of Eminent Philosophers* 3.1 (64) - apposite in relation to my idiosyncratic use of some Greek terms:

χρῆται δὲ ὁ Πλάτων ἐνίοτε αὐτῷ καὶ ἐπὶ τοῦ κακοῦ: ἔστι δ᾽ ὅτε καὶ ἐπὶ τοῦ μικροῦ. πολλάκις δὲ καὶ διαφέρουσιν ὀνόμασιν ἐπὶ τοῦ αὐτοῦ σημαινομένου χρῆται.

David Myatt
2015

[1] My translation, from *Ιερός Λόγος: An Esoteric Mythos. A Translation Of And A Commentary On The Third Tractate Of The Corpus Hermeticum.* 2015.

[2] Quidditas being 11th/12th century post-classical Latin, from whence derived the scholastic term 'quiddity'.

[3] *Towards Understanding Physis.* The essay in included in *Sarigthersa: Some Recent Essays.* 2015.

[4] "Although this naming and expression [which I explain] exists, human beings tend to ignore it, both before and after they have become aware of it. Yet even though, regarding such naming and expression, I have revealed details of how Physis has been cleaved asunder, some human beings are inexperienced concerning it, fumbling about with words and deeds, just as other human beings, be they interested or just forgetful, are unaware of what they have done."

The translation - together with the Greek text and a brief commentary - is included as an appendix to *Towards Understanding Physis.*

Appendix II

On Translating Ancient Greek

Given that I have numerous times over the past ten or so years been asked by various individuals (including Greek scholars) about my Greek translations, and given that it seems some of my translations (such as parts of the Corpus Hermeticum) are regarded as "iconoclastic and controversial", it seems fitting to provide a rather more detailed explanation of my methodology over and above my few, short, previous remarks.

When studying New Testament Greek while a monk in a Christian monastery in the 1970s - and being already familiar (from schooldays and later studies including at that monastery) with Homer's Greek and the way that Aeschylus often omitted 'the article' and invented new words to express his meaning - I began to wonder, in respect of translations, about what I have since termed 'retrospective re-interpretation'. As I mentioned in my essay *Some Examples*

Regarding Translation and Questions of Interpretation, included as an Appendix to my Poemandres translation and commentary:

> "I incline toward the view that in translations into English it is often best to avoid words that impose or seem to impose a meaning on an ancient text especially if the sense that an English word now imputes is the result of centuries of assumptions or opinions or influences and thus has acquired a modern meaning, or an interpretation, somewhat at variance with the culture, the milieu, of the time when the text that is being translated was written. Especially so in the matter of religious or spiritual texts where so many people rely or seem to rely on the translations, the interpretations, of others and where certain interpretations seem to have become fixed.
>
> Thus, it may be helpful if one can suggest, however controversial or iconoclastic they may seem in their time, reasoned alternatives for certain words important for a specific and a general understanding of a particular text, and helpful because such alternatives might enable a new appreciation of such a text, as if for instance one is reading it for the first time with the joy of discovery.
>
> For example, one of the prevalent English words used in translations of the New Testament, and one of the words now commonly associated with revealed religions such as Christianity and Islam, is sin. A word which now imputes and for centuries has imputed a particular and at times somewhat strident if not harsh moral attitude, with sinners starkly contrasted with the righteous and the saved, and with sin, what is evil, what is perverse, to be shunned and shudderingly avoided."

I then proceeded to give various quotations and argued that the original sense of the English word 'sin' was

> "the sense of doing what was wrong, of committing an error, of making a mistake, of being at fault; at most of overstepping the bounds, of transgressing limits imposed by others, and thus being 'guilty' of such an infraction, a sense which the suggested etymology of the word syn implies: from the Latin sons, sontis."

Hence why in translating John 8.7 I eschewed the much overused and now often pejorative word sin:

> So, as they continued to ask [for an answer] he straightened himself, saying to them: Let he who has never made a mistake [Αναμαρτητος] throw the first stone at her.
>
> ὡς δὲ ἐπέμενον ἐρωτῶντες αὐτόν, ἀνέκυψεν καὶ εἶπεν αὐτοῖς· ὁ

ἀναμάρτητος ὑμῶν πρῶτος ἐπ' αὐτὴν βαλέτω λίθον.

While such a translation may well be controversial, to me it imparts something important regarding the teachings, and the life, of Jesus of Nazareth: something quite human, something rather different from a stern preacher preaching about 'sin'; something which to me seems to express what the Beatitudes express, and something which individuals such as Julian of Norwich, George Fox and William Pen many centuries later tried to say and write about Christianity and about the teachings and the life of Jesus of Nazareth.

This seeking after meaning beyond what a particular English word now often denoted - in common usage or otherwise - I applied to my translations of some fragments of Heraclitus, to my translations of three tractates of the Corpus Hermeticum, and am applying to my on-going (as of 2016) translation of and commentary on the Gospel of John. I also used this principle, albeit then in a mostly intuitive way, when undertaking my translations, decades before, of Sophocles and Aeschylus.

Thus I saught to try and understand - to apprehend, both intuitively and by scholarly means - what the author was expressing or saught to express all those centuries ago; which necessitated understanding the milieu, the ethos, the culture, of the time and the place where the author lived. My approach was therefore more than strictly grammatical; more than lexicographical.

Why is why, in the Hermetic tractates the translation of such words as ἀγαθός and εὐσεβέω and θεός were considered in the necessary context. [1]

What, for example, did θεός mean and imply in the Hellenic times that the texts were written? My view is that to translate as 'god' is to miss the variety of possible meanings, since 'god' to so many people in the West imparts the sense of, if not the God of Christianity, then of 'the one deity' of neo-pythagoreanism and gnosticism. This then leads and has led to speculation as whether God and 'the one deity' are the same and whether the texts are neo-pythagorean and/or gnostic and/or possibly influenced by early Christianity. The texts under consideration, however, are unclear as to exactly what and who θεός is, especially given (i) that in the Poemandres tractate θεός is described as being both male and female (ἀρρενόθηλυς) and (ii) that 'archetypes'/deities from classical Greek culture are mentioned, from Psyche to Hermes, and (iii) that Poemandres is described as 'changing their form/appearance' (shapeshifting) in the manner of Greek divinities such as Athena in The Odyssey and Demeter in mythological poems and legends, and (iv) the mention of 'daimons'. This θεός might thus refer to a deity in a classical sense, with the texts describing a mysticism that is essentially a development of existing and past Greek ideas.

To translate θεός as god is therefore, in my view, not helpful given that 'god' is not, in our milieu, a neutral world and therefore tends to impose a certain meaning on the text. In contrast, the transliteration 'theos' is neutral and also aids the curiosity of the reader who might well then ask: what and who, here, is theos?

In regard to εὐσεβέω, is what is meant what we understand by terms such as reverent and pious? Again, given the influence of Christianity over the past two millennia, what such terms now so often denote is redolent of that religion so that such words are not neutral in respect of understanding the spirituality of such ancient Greek texts. Hence why my choice was for an expression: 'awareness of the numinous', which expression encompasses - or seems to me to encompass - an essential aspect of all spirituality, from ancient Greece to Greco-Roman times to Christianity and beyond. There is therefore, yet again, no retrospective re-interpretation of the text resulting from a poor choice of English words.

In considering ἀγαθός my basic guide was ἀγαθός contrasted with κακός in ancient Greece and Greco-Roman times with the sense being not some abstract god-given 'what is good' and 'what is evil', nor of some impersonal idea of 'good' contrasted with some other impersonal idea of 'evil', but rather the difference between good (noble) and bad (rotten) individuals, and which difference (according to so many authors of those times) was revealed, became known, through the deeds done by individuals. An interesting passage illustrating ἀγαθός contrasted with κακός occurs in section eight of the fourth tractate of the Corpus Hermeticum:

> τούτων δὲ οὕτως ἐχόντων, ὦ Τάτ, τὰ μὲν παρὰ τοῦ θεοῦ ἡμῖν τε ὑπῆρξε καὶ ὑπάρξει· τὰ δὲ ἀφ' ἡμῶν ἀκολουθησάτω καὶ μὴ ὑστερησάτω· ἐπεὶ ὁ μὲν θεὸς ἀναίτιος, ἡμεῖς δὲ αἴτιοι τῶν κακῶν, ταῦτα προκρίνοντες τῶν ἀγαθῶν

Nearly all past translations have opted to use the English words 'good' and 'evil', as did John Everard and G.R.S. Mead whose respective translations are,

> These things being so, O Tat, that things have been, and are so plenteously ministered to us from God; let them proceed also from us, without any scarcity or sparing. For God is innocent or guiltless, but we are the causes of Evil, preferring them before the Good.

> This being so, O Tat, what comes from God hath been and will be ours; but that which is dependent on ourselves, let this pressonward and have no delay; for 'tis not God, 'tis we who are the cause of evil things, preferring them to good.

A more recent translation is that of Brian Copenhaver,

> Since this is so, Tat, what proceeds from god has been and will be available to us. May what comes to us be suited to it and not deficient.

And the evils for which we are responsible, who chose them instead of good things, are no responsibility of god's.

In contrast, I interpret as,

> Because of this, then - Thoth - what is from theos can be and has been ours
> So let what accompanies us be that now instead of later.
> For it is we who select dishonour rather than honour
> With theos blameless in this.

Which interpretation emphasises the personal origin of what is done and why what is bad, in personal terms, is - as the author of the text later writes, αὕτη διαφορὰ τοῦ ὁμοίου πρὸς τὸ ἀνόμοιον, καὶ τῷ ἀνομοίῳ ὑστέρημα πρὸς τὸ ὅμοιον - a privation of what is good:

This is the distinction between what is akin and what is different With what is different having a privation of what is akin. Which contrast between personal honour (a nobility of character) and dishonour (a doing of rotten deeds) is rather different from abstract "evil things", and well expresses an important aspect of the ethos of ancient Greece and of Greco-Roman culture; an aspect well-expressed by Sophocles:

πόλεμος οὐδέν᾽ ἄνδρ᾽ ἑκὼν αἱρεῖ πονηρόν ἀλλὰ τοὺς χρηστοὺς ἀεί battle does not willingly take cowards, but - as of old - the honourable Philoctetes, v.437 This interpretation of ἀγαθός - in the personal terms of such an ethos, rather than as some abstract existent external to the individual as posited by Plato, ἡ τοῦ ἀγαθοῦ ἰδέα - is why the author of text also writes,

> ὁρᾷς, ὦ τέκνον, πόσα ἡμᾶς δεῖ σώματα διεξελθεῖν, καὶ πόσους χοροὺς δαιμόνων καὶ συνέχειαν καὶ δρόμους ἀστέρων ἵνα πρὸς τὸν ἕνα καὶ μόνον σπεύσωμεν; ἀδιάβατον γὰρ τὸ ἀγαθὸν καὶ ἀπέραντον καὶ ἀτελές, αὐτῷ δὲ καὶ ἄναρχον, ἡμῖν δὲ δοκοῦν ἀρχὴν ἔχειν τὴν γνῶσιν. οὐκ αὐτοῦ οὖν ἀρχὴ γίνεται ἡ γνῶσις
>
> Do you, my son, apprehend how many celestial bodies we have to traverse -
> How many groups of Daimons and sequential constellations -
> So that we hasten to the Monas.
> For the honourable is unpassable, without limit, and unending
> Even though to us its origin appears to be the knowledge.
> But even though such knowledge is not the origin of it
> It yields to us the origin of our knowing. [2]

For Plato's explanation requires a questioning, a philosophical search for ἀληθεία, a type of anados, resulting in a knowing of 'the good', ἡ τοῦ ἀγαθοῦ ἰδέα, and which knowing - which knowledge - is the source, the origin, of all other knowing. Here, the opposite is clearly stated: that such knowledge of 'the good', of what is honourable, is not 'the knowledge' - the conclusion of our anados - but instead only the source of what we know about ourselves and about others.

This understanding of 'the good', of ἀγαθός, is indeed somewhat controversial - the opposite of what Plato et al theorized and what some seem to have assumed regarding the Corpus Hermeticum - but one which presents an alternative (a somewhat paganus) understanding of such hermeticism as is described in the three tractates under consideration. And an interesting alternative that, to my knowledge, has been long neglected, given the various and the numerous assumptions made regarding the meaning of certain Greek words in texts such as the Corpus Hermeticum. [3]

David Myatt
2016

[1] In order to elucidate my methodology I for brevity only consider here three Greek terms.

[2] As I noted in my commentary on tractate IV:

> Reading ἀδιάβατον, which implies that what is honourable is always there, always around, always noticeable when it is presenced by someone. In other words - given the following καὶ ἀπέραντον καὶ ἀτελές - there are always some mortals who will (qv. sections 5 and 8) select honour rather than dishonour: who will (as described in section 4) "receive the perceiveration," having won that prize gifted by theos [...]
>
> The expression ἡμῖν δὲ δοκοῦν ἀρχὴν ἔχειν τὴν γνῶσιν is interesting given that it refers to 'the knowledge', which some have construed to refer to the gnosis of certain pagan weltanschauungen. However, since what this particular knowledge is, is not specified, to translate as 'the Gnosis' would be to impose a particular and modern interpretation on the text given what the term gnosticism now denotes. All that can be adduced from the text is that this particular knowledge may refer to and be the knowledge imparted in the text itself: the knowledge that Hermes is here imparting to Thoth.

[3] In respect of ἀγαθός, qv. Appendix III, *Concerning ἀγαθός and νοῦς in the Corpus Hermeticum*.

Appendix III

Concerning ἀγαθός and νοῦς in the Corpus Hermeticum

Three of the many Greek terms of interest in respect of understanding the varied weltanschauungen outlined in the texts that comprise the Corpus Hermeticum are ἀγαθός and νοῦς and θεός, with conventional translations of these terms as 'good' and 'Mind' and 'god' (or God) imparting the sense of reading somewhat declamatory sermons about god/God and 'the good' familiar from over a thousand years of persons preaching about Christianity interspersed with definitive philosophical statements about 'Mind', as if a "transcendent intelligence, rationality," or a "Mental or psychic faculty" or both, or something similar, is meant or implied.

Thus the beginning of tractate VI - τὸ ἀγαθόν, ὦ Ἀσκληπιέ, ἐν οὐδενί ἐστιν, εἰ μὴ ἐν μόνῳ τῷ θεῷ, μᾶλλον δὲ τὸ ἀγαθὸν αὐτός ἐστιν ὁ θεὸς ἀεί - and dealing as it does with both ἀγαθός and θεός, has been translated, by Mead, as "Good, O Asclepius, is in none else save God alone; nay, rather, Good is God Himself eternally," [1] and by Copenhaver as "The good, Asclepius, is in nothing except in god alone, or rather god himself is always the good." [2]

In respect of νοῦς, a typical example is from Poemandres 12 - ὁ δὲ πάντων πατὴρ ὁ Νοῦς, ὢν ζωὴ καὶ φῶς, ἀπεκύησεν Ἄνθρωπον αὐτῷ ἴσον, οὗ ἠράσθη ὡς ἰδίου τόκου· περικαλλὴς γάρ, τὴν τοῦ πατρὸς εἰκόνα ἔχων· ὄντως γὰρ καὶ ὁ θεὸς ἠράσθη τῆς ἰδίας μορφῆς, παρέδωκε τὰ ἑαυτοῦ πάντα δημιουργήματα. The beginning of this is translated by Mead as "But All-Father Mind, being Life and Light, did bring forth Man co-equal to Himself, with whom He fell in love, as being His own child for he was beautiful beyond compare," and by Copenhaver as "Mind, the father of all, who is life and light, gave birth to a man like himself whom he loved as his own child. The man was most fair: he had the father's image."

Similarly, in respect of Poemandres 22 - παραγίνομαι αὐτὸς ἐγὼ ὁ Νοῦς τοῖς ὁσίοις καὶ ἀγαθοῖς καὶ καθαροῖς καὶ ἐλεήμοσι, τοῖς εὐσεβοῦσι, καὶ ἡ παρουσία μου γίνεται βοήθεια, καὶ εὐθὺς τὰ πάντα γνωρίζουσι καὶ τὸν πατέρα ἱλάσκονται ἀγαπητικῶς καὶ εὐχαριστοῦσιν εὐλογοῦντες καὶ ὑμνοῦντες τεταγμένως πρὸς αὐτὸν τῇ στοργῇ - which is translated by Mead as "I, Mind, myself am present with holy men and good, the pure and merciful, men who live piously. [To such] my presence doth become an aid, and straightway they gain gnosis of all things, and win the Father's love by their pure lives, and give Him thanks, invoking on Him blessings, and chanting hymns, intent on Him with ardent love," and by Copenhaver as "I myself, the mind, am present to the blessed and good and pure and merciful - to the reverent - and my presence becomes a help; they quickly recognize everything, and they propitiate the father lovingly and give thanks, praising and singing hymns affectionately and in the order appropriate to him."

As explained in various places in my commentary on tractates I, III, IV, VIII, and XI, and in two appendices [3], I incline toward the view that - given what such English terms as 'the good', Mind, and god now impute, often as a result of two thousand years of Christianity and post-Renaissance, and modern, philosophy - such translations tend to impose particular and modern interpretations on the texts and thus do not present to the reader the ancient ethos that forms the basis of the varied weltanschauungen outlined in the texts of the Corpus Hermeticum.

To avoid such impositions, and in an endeavour to express at least something of that ancient (and in my view non-Christian) ethos, I have - for reasons explained in the relevant sections of my commentary - transliterated θεὸς as theos [4], νοῦς as perceiveration, or according to context, perceiverance; and ἀγαθός as, according to context, nobility, noble, or honourable [5]. Which is why my reading of the Greek of the three examples above provides the reader with a somewhat different impression of the texts:

° Asclepius, the noble exists in no-thing: only in theos alone; indeed, theos is, of himself and always, what is noble. [6]

° Perceiveration, as Life and phaos, father of all, brought forth in his own likeness a most beautiful mortal who, being his child, he loved.

° I, perceiveration, attend to those of respectful deeds, the honourable, the refined, the compassionate, those aware of the numinous; to whom my being is a help so that they soon acquire knowledge of the whole and are affectionately gracious toward the father, fondly celebrating in song his position.

But, as I noted in respect of ἀγαθός in the *On Ethos And Interpretation* appendix, whether these particular insights of mine are valid, others will have to decide. But they - and my translations of the tractates in general - certainly, at least in my fallible opinion, convey an impression about ancient Hermeticism which is rather different from that conveyed by other translations.

David Myatt
March 2017

o o o

Notes

[1] G.R.S Mead. *Thrice-Greatest Hermes*. Theosophical Society (London). 1906.

[2] B. Copenhaver. *Hermetica*. Cambridge University Press. 1992

[3] My translation of and commentary on tractates I, III, IV, and XI - and the two appendices - is available in pdf format at https://davidmyatt.wordpress.com/2017/03/08/corpus-hermeticum-i-iii-iv-xi/

My translation of and commentary on tractate VIII is available in pdf format at https://davidmyatt.wordpress.com/2017/03/20/corpus-hermeticum-viii/

[4] To be pedantic, when θεὸς is mentioned in the texts it often literally refers to 'the' theos so that at the beginning of tractate VI, for example, the reference is to 'the theos' rather than to 'god'.

[5] In respect of 'the good' - τὸ ἀγαθόν - as 'honourable', qv. Seneca, *Ad Lucilium Epistulae Morales*, LXXI, 4, "summum bonum est quod honestum est. Et quod magis admireris: unum bonum est, quod honestum est, cetera falsa et adulterina bona sunt."

[6] The suggestion seems to be that 'the theos' is the origin, the archetype, of what is noble, and that only through and because of theos can what is noble be presenced and recognized for what it is, and often recognized by those who are, or that which is, an eikon of theos. Hence why in tractate IV it is said that "the eikon will guide you,"; why in tractate XI that "Kosmos is the eikon of theos, Kosmos [the eikon] of Aion, the Sun [the eikon] of Aion, and the Sun [the eikon] of mortals," and why in the same tractate it is said that "there is nothing that cannot be an eikon of theos," and why in Poemandres 31 theos is said to "engender all physis as eikon."

As I noted in my commentary - qv. especially the mention of Maximus of Constantinople in respect of Poemandres 31 - I have transliterated εἰκὼν.

Appendix IV

Cicero On Summum Bonum

In *De Finibus Bonorum et Malorum* Marcus Tullius Cicero, in criticizing Epicurus and others, presents his view of Summum Bonum, a term normally translated as 'the supreme good'. According to Cicero, honestum (honourable conduct) is the foundation of Summum Bonum which itself can be discerned by careful consideration (*ratio*) in conjunction with that knowing (*scientia*) of what is divine and what is mortal that has been described as wisdom (sapientia).

> aequam igitur pronuntiabit sententiam ratio adhibita primum
> divinarum humanarumque rerum scientia, quae potest appellari rite
> sapientia, deinde adiunctis virtutibus, quas ratio rerum omnium

dominas, tu voluptatum satellites et ministras esse voluisti. (II, 37)

He then writes that honestum does not depend on any personal benefit (omni utilitate) that may result or be expected but instead can be discerned by means of consensus among the whole community in combination with the example afforded by the honourable actions and motives of the finest of individuals.

> Honestum igitur id intellegimus, quod tale est, ut detracta omni utilitate sine ullis praemiis fructibusve per se ipsum possit iure laudari. quod quale sit, non tam definitione, qua sum usus, intellegi potest, quamquam aliquantum potest, quam communi omnium iudicio et optimi cuiusque studiis atque factis, qui permulta ob eam unam causam faciunt, quia decet, quia rectum, quia honestum est, etsi nullum consecuturum emolumentum vident. (II, 45f)

In effect, Summum Bonum – what the Greeks termed τὸ ἀγαθὸν – depends on certain personal qualities such as a careful consideration of a matter; on a personal knowing of what is divine and what is mortal; on the example of personal noble deeds and motives, and on a communal consensus.

There is therefore nothing morally abstract or dogmatic about Cicero's understanding of Summum Bonum which so well expresses, as does Seneca [1], the Greco-Roman view, with a perhaps more apt translation of the term Summum Bonum thus being "the highest nobility".

David Myatt
2017

○ ○ ○

[1] "summum bonum est quod honestum est; et quod magis admireris: unum bonum est, quod honestum est, cetera falsa et adulterina bona sunt". Ad Lucilium Epistulae Morales, LXXI, 4

Appendix IV

Swan Song Of A Mystic?
by Rachael Stirling

The latest effusion from Mr David Myatt, titled *Some Questions For DWM 2017*, is interesting for a variety of reasons not least of which is that it is permeated – as is his philosophy of pathei-mathos – with references to the classical culture of ancient Greece and Rome. It is also – perhaps unintentionally – revealing about Myatt's character providing as it does facts about his life and how he now views his philosophy of pathei-mathos, which philosophy he has previously described as his weltanschauung, his own outlook on life.

The overall impression is of a man steeped in Western culture who is still ineluctably part of that culture but who – even though already withdrawn from the world – desires as a mystic might to cut what few ties still bind him to the world of vanity and materialism.

The Philosophy of Pathei Mathos

One of these ties appears to be his philosophy of pathei-mathos. This is a philosophy which is not only clearly pagan and part of the Western philosophical tradition but also one which provides we Westerners with a cultured – a philosophical – paganism relevant to the modern world which is completely different from and even at odds with what has been termed both "contemporary paganism" and "neopaganism" with its invented rituals and ceremonies, its belief in and revival of ancient deities, and its lack of philosophical rigour. In effect, Myatt has continued, refined, and evolved the Western paganism – the ancient, the classical, paganism – evident in the works Homer, Hesiod, Aeschylus, Cicero, the Corpus Hermeticum, and Marcus Aurelius, stripping away the old idea of gods and goddesses and replacing them with a modern mysticism centred around philosophical concepts such as Being and physis {2}, and virtues such as personal honour, pathei mathos, and empathy. Such a philosophical approach also conveniently does away – sans polemics – with conventional religions such as Christianity. {3}

Why then – given this gift to those seeking a Western alternative to the likes of Christianity who are unable to take "contemporary paganism" and "neopaganism" seriously – does Myatt in his latest effusion seem, as some have commented, to reject his own pagan philosophy? For among other things he writes,

"All that 'philosophy' seems to be to me now is a rather wordy and a rather egoistic, vainful, attempt to present what I (rightly or wrongly) believed I had learned about myself and the world as a result of various experiences."

My own view is that he is not rejecting that philosophy, only moving on, as a composer of musical works – finding themselves unsatisfied with their creations – moves on to other things, to new compositions. In other words, Myatt is only re-expressing what he said some years ago, which was that the philosophy of pathei-mathos was

"simply my own weltanschauung, a weltanschauung developed over some years as a result of my own pathei-mathos. Thus, and despite whatever veracity it may or may not possess, it is only the personal insight of one very fallible individual." {4}

In Myatt's case he is simply moving on to concentrate on translations, and to live as his conscience dictates, or rather as his own pathei mathos informs him he should, which is life as a modern recluse and a learned mystic.

That he is not rejecting his own philosophy but instead is just not going to write anymore about it – or as he says, is not going to "pontificate" about it anymore – is evident in two of his replies. For in one reply he writes "I would suggest the tentative answers expressed by my weltanschauung," while in another that such philosophical essays "can be, and in my case seem to have been, manifestations of vanity."

But whether he will really write no more philosophical essays remains to be seen for there have been many writers, artists and musicians who, having forsworn their craft, nevertheless return to it at some stage.

A Western Heritage

In his latest effusion Myatt acknowledges his Western heritage, writing that as a schoolboy he read in Greek the likes of Thucydides, Homer, Plato, Aristotle, and Herodotus, and in a rather remarkable admission that what he

> "imbibed in those early years from such books of Ancient Hellas was nothing particularly philosophical but instead martial, and I could not but help admire those 'thinking warriors', those 'perspicacious inventive gentlemen' (περιφραδὴς ἀνήρ as Sophocles described them, cunning in inventive arts who arrive now with dishonour and then with honour, τι τὸ μηχανόεν τέχνας ὑπὲρ ἐλπίδ'ἔχων τοτὲ μὲν κακόν, ἄλλοτ' ἐπ' ἐσθλὸν ἕρπει) nurtured as I was then and had been for years by and in various colonies and outposts of what was still the British Empire. Thus it was natural that when, a short time later, I first learned about the Third Reich and about the loyalty of a soldier such as Otto Ernst Remer and the heroic actions of warriors such as Leon Degrelle I admired such men and intuited that something of the warrior ethos of ancient Hellas and Sparta may have manifested itself in our modern world."

He also admits that

> "some aspects of some of the tractates of the Corpus Hermeticum have influenced my thinking, just as Aristotle, Aeschylus, Sophocles, Marcus Aurelius, and other classical and Hellenistic Greek and Latin writers have."

That he does not mention any non-Western literature I find indicative.

Thus it is my view that Myatt – despite some of his past peregrinations or perhaps because of some of those peregrinations – is still rooted in and still contributing to the ethos of the West, a fact evident in his philosophy of pathei-mathos and also in his on-going translations of texts from the Corpus Hermeticum and his on-going translation of the Gospel of John, both of which are important for understanding the past and the current ethos of the West itself particularly as Myatt notes, in one of his replies, that his presumption is "of early Christianity probably being influenced by the diverse hermetic traditions which existed and flourished during the Hellenistic period."

This rootedness in the culture of the West is also evident in another of his replies, with Myatt lamenting that

> "for so many in the modern West there is no longer an ancestral culture of which one is a living, dwelling, part – a connexion between the past and the future and a connexion with a rural place of dwelling – and which culture preserves the slowly learned wisdom of the past."

Like a few others, my view is that his philosophy of pathei-mathos as well as his translations provide some of the links we need to reconnect ourselves with our Western ancestral culture.

Rachael Stirling
August 2017

{1} In one of his replies Myatt writes that in his philosophy

> "the apparent parts of the unity are expressed by descriptors such as masculous and muliebral, with that unity – The One, μονάς – not designated by terms such as theos (God, god) or theoi (gods) but rather metaphysically, as Being and the emanations/effluvia of Being such as ourselves, Nature, and the Cosmos itself."

{2} A detailed analysis of Myatt's philosophy is given in the 2016 book *The Mystic Philosophy Of David Myatt*.

{3} *The Way Of Pathei-Mathos – A Précis*. The essay is in the 2014 compilation titled *One Vagabond In Exile From The Gods: Some Personal and Metaphysical Musings*.

Appendix VI

Self-Dramatization, Sentimentalist, Or Chronicler Of Pathei Mathos?

Overview: Personal Effusions

Many of David Myatt's post-2006 writings are intensely personal. In particular, the letters - or extracts from private letters - which he has published are full of personal feelings, such as in the following examples; the first from his *The Joy-bringing Sky-blue*, written in 2006, and the second from his *One Error-Prone Self* written in 2012, with both included in his 2013 book

Understanding and Rejecting Extremism.

> « So I am haunted, here and again, where again the Swallows gather as they gather at this time of year: chirping to each other and preparing in some weeks to leave. Thus do they skim the fields, catching, eating, their food as
> the cycle of natural life upwardly repeats and a cooling breeze dims a little of the humid heat of the day, here in a greening part of a still-living England. Haunted, here and again – amid such joyful growing warmth – with, by, because of, her death; with by, because of, the multiplicity of my multitudes of suffering-causing and so stupid mistakes. »

> « There is a certain inner emptiness, and often, and bearing grief and sadness, when alone indoors. Inner vacant sometimes colding spaces which perhaps a belief in God - or the gods - might fill, and which certainly a partner or prayer or both would warm and dissipate. Yet this certain inner emptiness, such sadness, I sense is perhaps is as it should be for me, as part expiation for the varied harm my varied pasts - in this one life - have caused [.....] But I have no chanted, sung, or contemplative Opus Dei to try, in monastic peace and with hope and faith, to balance - Soli Deo Honor et Gloria - the unwise deeds of so many; nor any longer a desire or need to interfere in the lives of others. So there is for me only the living of each moment as it passes: no aim, no goal. »

The overall impression is of reading someone's private diary, with there being so many published emotive and personal effusions over so many years naturally leading us to ask pertinent questions about Myatt himself. Why publish what many people will undoubtedly dismiss - or already have dismissed - as either mawkish or as self-dramatization or as both, and do such published personal effusions detract from both his translations and his philosophy of pathei mathos? There is also, of course, given his extremist past and given particular allegations about him and the Occult, the obvious question of whether the feelings expressed in these outpourings are genuine particularly as Myatt appears to have ready-made answers to such questions. Such as this, from his *Some Questions For DWM 2017*,

> « My only - quite feeble - excuse for the plenitude of such post-2011 writings is that they, through the act of writing and corresponding with others, were partly expiative but mostly aided (or seemed to me to aid) my understanding of myself particularly in relation to my extremist past and the religions I had personal and practical experience of. »

Or this, from his earlier *Some Questions For DWM 2014*,

> « My writings, post-2011, were and are really dialogues: interiorly

with myself and externally with a few friends or the occasional person who has contacted me and expressed an interest. They are just my attempts to answer particular philosophical and metaphysical questions which interest or perplex me; attempts to understand myself and my extremist past (and thus understand extremism itself), and attempts to express what I believe I have, via pathei-mathos, come to understand and appreciate. Thus, I make no claims regarding the worth or the importance of these personal and philosophical musings, with such dialogues, musings, and correspondence published mostly because expiatory but also because (being honest) of vanity in the hope that some of them may possibly, just possibly, be of some interest to a few individuals interested in such philosophical and metaphysical questions or interested in understanding extremism and its causes. But if no one takes them seriously, it does not matter, for they have assisted me in understanding myself, in recognizing and acknowledging my past mistakes and the suffering I have caused, and aided my move from extremism toward developing a mystical and personal weltanschauung imbued with a muliebral ethos. »

An Assessment

The sheer quantity of material - amounting to hundreds of published letters and essays dating from 2006 to 2017 - is a good starting point. Arranging them into date order, beginning with his *The Scent of Meadow Grass* {1} written in 2006 "four days on from Fran's death" and ending with his *Some Questions For DWM 2017*, they tell a particular personal story. A story which includes works such as *Religion, Empathy, and Pathei-Mathos: Essays and Letters Regarding Spirituality, Humility, and A Learning From Grief* {2} and, of course, his 'autobiography' - his apologia - titled *Myngath* {3}.

The personal story that is told by this material is that of an arrogant, violent, fanatic who spent thirty years as a neo-nazi activist, ideologue, and propagandist, followed by ten years as a radical Muslim preaching Jihad and who publicly supported al-Qaida, Hamas, and 'suicide attacks'. Which - with his various terms of imprisonment for violence, his leadership of a gang of thieves, his terrorist manual which inspired the London nail-bomber, followed by his conversion to Islam - is itself an interesting if strange story had it ended with him, for example, in prison as a Muslim for such offences as 'inviting support for a proscribed organisation', or 'possessing a document containing information likely to be useful to a person committing or preparing an act of terrorism' or 'inciting terrorism overseas'.

But the story did not end with his Muslim years. He suffered a personal tragedy, the unexpected suicide in 2006 of his fiancée and which tragedy maybe for the first time in his life grounded him in the realities of human suffering and grief. According to his post-2006 personal writings {4} it was this singular event which caused him to reflect upon his extremist past and upon him own character.

In a long letter dated March 2010 and to which letter he gave the title *One More Foolish Failure* Myatt wrote

> « I am such a fool; such a failure, in evolutionary terms, in the perspective of the Cosmos. Here I am, entering the sixth decade of my life, having spent the last forty years seeking experience and wisdom and having, in that time, made so many errors, mistakes, and been the cause of much suffering, personal and otherwise. How then can I be deemed wise? How - when I have leant, from sorrowful experience, from my own pathei-mathos, from the personal tragedy of the dying and the death of two loved ones, and yet have always always, until now, returned to pursuing suffering-causing abstractions and unethical goals?
>
> There is no excuse for this failure of mine, year following year - although of course I have always made excuses for myself, as failures often do. Wordy, moral-sounding, inexcusable excuses almost always of the unethical "the end justifies the means" kind.
>
> No excuses - because from sorrow, from personal tragedy, I felt, dis-covered, the unethical nature of all abstractions, be they deemed political, religious, or social. And yet I always seemed, until a month ago, to gravitate back toward them, as if there was some basic flaw in my personal nature, my character, that allowed or even caused such a return, such a stupid forgetting of lessons learnt [.....]
>
> Thus is there the same old haunting question - of how long will it be before I in my addiction forget The Numen, yet again, and so return to the suffering-causing habits of so many previous years? For now, I can only hope against hope that I have strength enough, memories enough, humility enough, to keep me where I know I should belong: infused, suffused, with the world of the numinous, enabling thus such an empathic living as can make us and keep us as ethical, compassionate, human beings; one sign toward the higher human type we surely have the potential to become. » {5}

It seems from subsequent writings that it was such feelings, such personal reflections, which spurred him to refine his then still incomplete 'numinous way' into what became his 'philosophy of pathei-mathos' {6} and in which philosophy personal humility plays a central role {7}. Which is probably why he wrote that

> « any Way or religion which manifests, which expresses, which guides

> individuals toward, the numinous humility we human beings need is good, and should not be stridently condemned. For such personal humility – that which prevents us from committing hubris, whatever the raison d'être, the theology, the philosophy – is a presencing of the numinous. Indeed, one might write and say that it is a personal humility – whatever the source – that expresses our true developed (that is, rational and empathic) human nature. » {8}

Myatt's story thus ends with this philosophy; with him - post-2012 - emphasizing again and again the virtues of humility, personal love, compassion, tolerance, and personal honour, and being emphatic that his philosophy involves a personal, a mystical, approach to life and therefore is neither political nor involves any religious dogmatism and presents only his answers to particular questions, writing in 2012 that

> « All I have are some personal and fallible answers to certain philosophical, personal, ethical, and theological, questions. No certainty about anything except about my own uncertainty of knowing and about the mistakes, the errors, of my past. » {9}

Two years later he wrote that

> « In a very personal sense, my philosophy of pathei-mathos is expiative. » {10}

Which theme of a personal expiation runs through all his post-2010 writings.

A Personal Conclusion

My assessment, based on the personal material Myatt has published since 2006, is that there is a definite narrative and that this narrative is emotionally, personally, and philosophically consistent. That these writings are not mawkish and certainly not the self-dramatization of someone seeking to draw attention to themselves. That they are in fact documenting the interior, the personal, struggles of someone trying to reform - to radically change - themselves following a personal tragedy; someone using such writings, and in particular their publication, as acts of both self-learning and expiation, with it being plausible that he used such publication as a reminder to both others and himself so that he could never again return to the selfishness and extremism of his past.

For documenting such a struggle - from neo-nazi to modern mystic - Myatt should be commended with his post-2006 personal writings and his philosophy of pathei mathos a contribution to what Myatt has termed our 'human culture of pathei-mathos' which he defined in his 2014 essay *Education And The Culture Of Pathei-Mathos* {11} as

> « the accumulated pathei-mathos of individuals, world-wide, over

thousands of years, as (i) described in memoirs, aural stories, and historical accounts; as (ii) have inspired particular works of literature or poetry or drama; as (iii) expressed via non-verbal mediums such as music and Art, and as (iv) manifest in more recent times by art-forms such as films and documentaries. »

Yet, and to paraphrase Myatt, it is not important if his post-2010 personal writings are not taken seriously by others since they enabled him to understand himself, acknowledge his mistakes, and reform himself.

J.B.
2017

{1} Included in the book *Understanding and Rejecting Extremism: A Very Strange Peregrination*. 2013. ISBN 978-1484854266
{2} Published in 2013. ISBN 978-1484097984. When publishing his letters or extracts therefrom Myatt often provides a title for individual letters.
{3} Published in 2013. ISBN 978-1484110744
{4} For example see the section titled *A Personal Tragedy* in *Myngath*, and also his collection of essays titled *Meditations on Extremism, Remorse, and The Numinosity of Love* published in 2016.
{5} The letter, too long to quote in full here, is worth reading in its entirely. It is included in *Meditations on Extremism, Remorse, and The Numinosity of Love*, and can be read on-line at https://davidmyatt.wordpress.com/one-more-foolish-failure/ [Accessed October 2017]
{6} See his 2012 essay *The Development of the Numinous Way*, included as an appendix in both *Myngath* and *Meditations on Extremism, Remorse, and The Numinosity of Love*.
{7} The role of humility in Myatt's philosophy is mentioned in Part Two of *An Overview of David Myatt's Philosophy of Pathei-Mathos* by R. Parker included in the book *The Mystic Philosophy Of David Myatt* published in 2015, ISBN 978-1523930135.
{8} *Soli Deo Gloria*, written in 2011. Can be read on-line at https://davidmyatt.wordpress.com/soli-deo-gloria/ [Accessed October 2017]
{9} From the 2012 letter - titled *Politics, Pathei-Mathos, and My Extremist Past* - included in Part Three of *Understanding and Rejecting Extremism*.
{10} *Some Questions For DWM 2014*.
{11} The essay is included in his book *One Vagabond In Exile From The Gods: Some Personal and Metaphysical Musings*, published in 2014. ISBN 978-1502396105

cc David Wulstan Myatt 2011-2017 & T.W.S. 2017

Second Edition

This work is licensed under the Creative Commons
(Attribution--NoDerivs 4.0) License
and can be copied and distributed according to the terms of that license.

All translations by David Myatt

Made in the USA
Columbia, SC
09 October 2024